# COSMIC ORDERING

## THE NEXT ADVENTURE

D1146690

Also by Barbel Mohr

*The Cosmic Ordering Service*

# COSMIC ORDERING

## THE NEXT ADVENTURE

## BARBEL MOHR

Translated from the German by Dawn Bailiff

HODDER
MOBIUS

Copyright © 1999 by Omega-Verlag

Translated into English by Dawn Bailiff

First published in Great Britain in 2007 by Hodder & Stoughton
A division of Hodder Headline

The right of Barbel Mohr to be identified as the Author
of the Work has been asserted by her in accordance with the
Copyright, Designs and Patents Act 1988.

A Mobius paperback

2

A CIP catalogue record for this title
is available from the British Library

ISBN 978 0 340 93333 6

Printed and bound by Mackays of Chatham Ltd, Chatham, Kent

Hodder Headline's policy is to use papers that are natural,
renewable and recyclable products and made from wood grown in
sustainable forests. The logging and manufacturing processes are expected
to conform to the environmental regulations of the country of origin.

Hodder & Stoughton Ltd
A division of Hodder Headline
338 Euston Road
London NW1 3BH

The story, "Dispatch from the Beyond" in Chapter 18
is quoted from the book, *Unglaubliche Geschicten* (Fantastic Stories)
by Pierre Bellemare, translated by France Brifaut.
Copyright © 1989 by nymphenburger in
der F. A. Herbig Verlagsbuchhandlung GmbH, Munich.

# Table of Contents

Good morning. Here, the universe speaks:

*Today, I will assume the burden of all your problems.*
*What's more, I will not need your help.*
*So, sit back and enjoy your day!*

# Preface

Dear Reader,

This is my second book in the Cosmic Ordering Service series. The first was entitled simply *The Cosmic Ordering Service*.

It does not matter which book you read first, for both equally offer the potential to fulfill your deepest desires, to increase your zest for life . . . to manifest miracles. Both books detail a simple and ingenious method for making your dreams come true.

Here again, I am addressing the lazy spiritualist, who like me, cannot muster the effort to exert great influence, but still wants to realize his/her dreams.

In contrast to the previous book, this work deals more with conscious, structured, long-term orders than with single, spontaneous requests for success.

Nonetheless, we will—in the name of "jolly good fun"—again place a few raucously single-minded demands.

Always, I wish you "Good Ordering," so that your inner light may guide your choices for the enrichment of us all!

Yours truly,
Barbel

# From Armani to Dirty Jeans and Back Again

If you have not read my first book, nor offered up one single order to the universe, you may, at first, wonder what this Cosmic Ordering Service is all about. Quite simply, it is best illustrated by the story "From Armani to Dirty Jeans and Back Again."

It all began in 1994, when Ingrid's highly successful husband (with a penchant for Giorgio Armani suits) had a serious car accident from which he did not recover. Actually, his body had recovered in six months; however, his mind— even after four years—had not recovered sufficiently for him to regain his professional status.

Meanwhile, one might say that the family went "from Armani to dirty jeans." Along with the financial pressures came marital discord, and Ingrid began to prepare her daughter for what seemed like an inevitable separation. Since her husband continued to remain unemployed, Ingrid knew she must look for work. Yet, after filling out over seventy applications, the best she could do was a single part-time job, two days a week for only a few hours a shift. This did not go far in supporting her entire family!

At the end of last year, Ingrid allowed herself, for the first time in quite awhile, to be persuaded to attend a party. When the time came, she went, admittedly, more because she had already promised than from a desire to go.

During the party, she found herself among the group of smokers on the balcony. There, another smoker, named Isabella, caught her attention. The two got into a conversation, in which Ingrid told Isabella that she admired her radiance and her temperament. She was even a bit jealous because her own life was a failure—her marriage, her job, simply everything.

Isabella, who was always a source of helpful information, immediately thought: this calls for an order to the universe. Although she was not certain whether this stranger before her would connect with this seemingly outlandish method, her thought intensified until she had to verbalize it: "Ingrid, I believe, you should call on the Cosmic Ordering Service."

"If you knew how many spiritual fanatics I have turned a deaf ear to," Ingrid sighed.

Yet, Isabella persisted: "I don't speak from a fanatical perspective but from a practical one! You think in concrete terms about what you would like to have, and then you send this order out in thought, trusting that what you desire already belongs to you."

Ingrid looked a little doubting, but Isabella was not finished with her remarks: "And don't order the same thing tomorrow. If you order something from the Source, you do not re-order it the next day. Otherwise, they think you are somewhat confused and send you nothing more at all."

Ingrid found that last sentence so funny that she decided it might be amusing to follow this peculiar advice at the next opportunity.

The party continued, and Ingrid did not return home until 2:30 A.M. Once there, she still had to walk the family dog. The beautiful, starry night fed her imagination, making her more receptive to the new ideas she had heard earlier, so she decided it would not be a bad idea to give this whole Cosmic Ordering Service a try. She recalled Isabella's instructions and considered, in detail, everything she would like to have.

Most importantly, she needed a better-paying job that she could coordinate with the care of their daughter. In addition, something had to happen in their marriage.

Her body and soul were so invested in these thoughts that her entire energy seemed to collect itself in her solar plexus and begin to circle there.

When she finally sent the order into the clear, starlit sky, it was as though a spiral emanated from the center of her being. It was nearly a mystical experience for Ingrid. She did not give it too much thought, but it was a little disconcerting, nonetheless.

The next day, she arrived at her part-time job. First thing in the morning, the telephone rang. It was their tax advisor, inquiring whether Ingrid was still looking for work. Ingrid admitted that she was. The tax advisor then gave her the number of a lady whose bookkeeper had abruptly quit some months ago, triggering a frantic search for a replacement which, so far, had turned up nothing.

Ingrid immediately called the lady and went for an interview that very afternoon. She could hardly believe it! Everyone in the office was very nice, and Ingrid and the owner clearly saw eye-to-eye. The only question that remained was: When could she start? "How about tomorrow?" the owner asked.

"No problem," said Ingrid, attempting to contain her excitement.

"Well, marvelous!" was the response. "I'll see you tomorrow."

How easy it can be! Ingrid was completely inspired. Upon arriving home, she immediately called Isabella, telling her that the first order had already appeared. The first call on the next morning after the order had already developed into a new job! Isabella was just as inspired.

The following day, Ingrid's husband—who had also been initiated in the Cosmic Ordering Service—called her at work: "Your next partial order has arrived. Despite your losses in the stock market, somehow, the final outcome is a credit of over $6,000!"

Nonsense, thought Ingrid, convinced that this simply could not be. "You must have misunderstood," she told her husband. "That is not possible! Fax the letter so I can see it. Surely, what is being called a plus is really a minus!"

Well, it was after all, a plus.

Meanwhile, their nine-year-old daughter began to catch on, successfully ordering some really nice small things. Naturally, she could not keep it to herself and so told her grandmother at the next opportunity: "Grandma, Mommy is now ordering with the universe, and everything comes, too . . ."

Ingrid's husband looked comfortably on but remained passive. Thanks to the Cosmic Ordering Service, Ingrid was now too strong and courageous to remain entrenched in the old life patterns. So, she gave her husband an ultimatum: "Either you undertake something by the first of December that I can recognize as a contribution to this family, or I take our daughter and go."

This was no idle threat, for Ingrid was determined to stand her ground. She had had enough of *Waiting for Godot*. It was clear that she expected more from the future than to live in constant fear of ruin.

On the first of December, Ingrid's husband informed her that he would start work the next day. He had a new job—as a truck driver! Ingrid's heart sank. She found it hard to believe that her Dapper Dan, so enamored of his fine suits and ties, could be content in dirty jeans, transporting goods to and fro until late in the evening.

Even though he doesn't come home before 9:00 P.M. and is completely wiped out, he is better than he has been in a long time. Finally, something interests him and he is earning money again, even if not very much. But most importantly, he is finally back in the swing of life.

As a result, Ingrid regained respect for her husband, rekindling that old spark. The two are, once again, happy in the marriage—to the joy of their small daughter.

It works like this: as soon as one can break free from the rigidity of old negative patterns, satisfaction with daily life can prevail, which in turn, regenerates creative ideas and initiative. For example, Ingrid's husband now leafs eagerly through the newspaper, considering how he can jump-start his career. Perhaps being a truck driver is merely a stepping-stone to help him get back on his feet, not the ideal course for him, long-term.

Well, this is pretty typical of how the Cosmic Ordering Service works. Does it all make sense? If not, then you still have most of this book left to inspire you. And in chapter 5, the exact technique of how to place orders is explained.

Naturally, some will object: perhaps, it was all a coincidence—Ingrid going right to the perfect new job, etc. But even if that were the case, so what? If one can draw enough fortitude from his or her faith in the power of the Cosmic Ordering Service to create positive life changes, the outcome is no less marvelous!

Furthermore, you take a big risk not trying the Cosmic Ordering Service, if it does in fact work. Why, everything wonderful may elude you! Whereas, you lose nothing by trying it out, playing around with it a bit, until miracles begin to pile up in your life.

# The Latest on the
# Cosmic Ordering Service

First I would like to give some introductory tips for new or up-to-now persistently unsuccessful orderers and report the latest on my own successes and failures.

What makes this difficult is that I give up my orders with childlike trust and directly forget about them.

It is obvious, with whom and when orders work especially well. Everything which one orders in ease and without attachment immediately comes forth. The more happy-go-lucky or naïve a person is, the more quickly he/she is likely to receive results upon sending this initial "test-order." Seemingly unfair, this runs contrary to the confirmed esoteric philosophy that how much one accomplishes is in direct proportion to how much one comprehends.

According to this belief system, ordering would take place in solemnity, and the matter would become entirely too important. This goes against the very nature of the process. Even worse: one believes to need something and hopes and worries that it will really come. Yet, nothing happens. Strange universal law, isn't it? He that needs something doesn't get it, while he that, for the sheer fun of it—almost as a game—orders something admittedly unnecessary, gets it immediately! Where is the divine justice in that?

Are we not created in "God's image," becoming creators in our own right, manifesting in our life that which we think and feel? It becomes clear: that which one fears, is the first thing that appears. And the more one worries, the more reasons for worry arise. The more lightheartedly one dances through life, the more easily things flow to him or her, almost like in the Land of Milk and Honey.

It is the creative force, inherent in each one of us, of which we must become fully aware. Our greatest danger lies in negative thoughts and feelings. Our greatest fear, therefore, must be of our own negative thinking, as it creates our reality.

Let me give you an example of an unconscious, negative order that I recently made, which, fortunately, I was able to alter.

I had gotten myself all worked up over the fact that, this year, due to fewer write-offs, I would have to pay more taxes.

Since I am inclined to spend everything that is in my account, I was afraid of receiving a bill that was higher than what I could pay.

So, I therefore, quite craftily, wrote the tax office, requesting to make an estimated tax prepayment. Thus, I imagined, I would not have to pay in one lump sum, who knows how much, later on. It was the perfect unconscious order—or so it seemed.

Complications arose immediately. The income tax office does not know which folks have to make estimated tax payments. It only noticed that I wanted to change something, and the prepayment was set to zero. Super! Naturally, I did not place much stock in this and nervously agreed to pay a lump sum of $13,000, which included the taxes for one year and the current prepayment. My fears had been realized.

But one can take countermeasures at any time. There probably was something of a "higher-consciousness" order due, since I had previously imagined and ordered money for myself. I told the universe that debts would not have to occur in my reality, not even with the tax office. Therefore, please send me money by the payment due date. On the one hand, I half believed that it could work out, since I dismissed debt as a necessary reality; however, on the other hand, the situation seemed to me, nevertheless, fraught with difficulty. The long and the short of it: two days before the payment was due, money flowed in from all directions. Unexpected commissions from recommendations, the pay back of money I had lent and no longer expected to see, etc. I had, admittedly, overdrawn my account by $5,200; however, I was still able to pay the taxes.

Extremely proud of what I perceived to be a successful order, I called my friend, Carsten, and told him all about it.

"Therefore, Baaarbel," he chided. "Now, read your own books for once! What are you doing with a minus $5,200 on the account? Why not a surplus of $30,000! You remember, that's the way it goes. What's the difference? So, really now!"

Immediately, my conscience nagged me. Although I give others good advice, I only practice it half-heartedly. Hmmm.

Nonetheless, I took away from this a valuable lesson: I suddenly realized how to make my orders more successful. Part of this actually consisted of abandoning the subject of money for four weeks because I secretly thought I shouldn't create this anyway. For most people, money is a difficult topic. Generally, only those that have enough money are successful at ordering up more.

Then Carsten paid me a visit (he lives 250 kilometers away), and I was filled with a sense of reproach that I don't stick to my own advice. Therefore, I ordered: "Dear Universe, today, Carsten is coming. Please send $35,000 by this evening."

Nothing happened. But I was lucky: Carsten seemed to have forgotten the whole thing. On the second evening, we were sitting in the kitchen when the telephone rang. It was my eighty-two-year-old aunt. She told me about a program that she had seen on television concerning inheritance taxes, which had greatly upset her. In order to avoid the inheritance tax, she had transferred $35,000 over to me that very day. I nearly fainted, and Carsten also looked greatly affected. Later, he acknowledged with amazement how quickly I put advice to good use.

As a result, he immediately recommended that I order a new car. First of all, I was beginning to really need one, and secondly, his suggestions seemed to work well. Three months later, I was given a new car as a gift. This time, not from a relative, but Carsten was again present at the scene, and we were both speechless. I see Carsten only every two to three months. That he participated in each of these "miracles" is a miracle in and of itself!

From all of this, I concluded that I think too many negative thoughts (concerns that I cannot pay the taxes or that it could be difficult, etc.). Fortunately, I have Carsten to pep me up at the right moment.

I have, however, also succeeded in pepping up Carsten. Once, I called him and told him about some particularly successful orders in the employment arena. We both make our living through freelance activities. As a result, Carsten was totally inspired and wanted to place an order right away, since he still had no clients for the coming week. We hung up, and a half-hour later, he called back, brimming with enthusiasm: "Barbel, you're not going to believe this, but the order has already been delivered! After I had given up the order, I took my trash down to the dumpster. There, I ran into my next-door neighbor, and we struck up a conversation about work. It turns out, he has a need for exactly what I do. Now, I have a super assignment for next week. An outstanding order. Hooray!"

In my circle of acquaintances, there were naturally malcontents, who upon hearing the above history, countered: "We have no rich aunts; therefore, this would not have worked for us." They did not seem to find it strange that my aunt called me a day after the order, offering the exact amount requested.

I reminded them of the time when I had ordered a somewhat higher sum and consequently found a job—the only time in my life when I was a salaried employee, for four months. The shop went out of business, and I received the balance of the ordered amount as a severance package. This can happen to everyone, except, of course, the doubters because they only work at "solid" companies.

Here is another example of bad turning to good: a lawyer in the U.S. ordered a new car and made a $10,000 down payment. Then, the delivery date of the car was postponed indefinitely. After six months, he finally bought another car from another manufacturer and demanded his $10,000 back, plus interest.

The automobile manufacturer reimbursed the $10,000, but refused—after many confrontations—to pay interest on the money they had held. This exasperated the lawyer, and he went to court. The judge found that the automobile company had tied up the credit limit of its customer interest free, and thus the customer should now be entitled to use the credit limit of the company. This amounted to 200 billion U.S. dollars, all of which the lawyer, according to the court order, would be allowed to borrow free of charge.

Of course, this did not please the company. After going back and forth, they finally paid the customer a tidy settlement instead of honoring the court decision. With this settlement, he could have bought himself an entire fleet—a windfall from heaven!

Here's a thought: you have ordered money for yourself. Did it ever occur to you that the universe could send it in such a way?

The stubborn doubters, of course, present new objections: they are not lawyers, and furthermore, such a thing can only happen in America, not in Germany. Now, they have a choice: if they prefer to cling to their negative thought patterns, nothing good can happen. Just as easily, they could think: "Perhaps there is a method to the madness. From all this, one can actually conclude that the universe will always intervene, and that it will also generate for me a creative idea, which I may not comprehend and fortunately do not need to comprehend. I order, and how the universe supplies, is its business."

It is within your power to avoid unconscious orders and unwanted deliveries, while continuing, with resolution, on the path of self-discovery. At some point (perhaps in one of your next two hundred to three hundred lives or in this one—however it comes) you will choose the ideal circumstances in your life to manifest from an awareness higher than thought. . . .

To achieve this, however, it is of the utmost importance that you conduct an accurate self-assessment, and the next chapter will help you do just that.

# Know Yourself

Every human being has the potential for a happy and fulfilling life. In order to achieve this, however, you must truly "know yourself."

I would like to illustrate this truth with a simple metaphor: if you were a sheep and went to a school that taught how to become a good wolf, what do you think your chances of success and happiness would be? Not too good, right? Failure is preordained. If, on the other hand, you went to school to learn how to be a better sheep, then you could become truly happy and successful. You would also end up dealing more effectively with wolves, since you would be operating from a position of confidence.

In order to know, right now, what in life will truly make you happy, you must first know who you are. Otherwise, you will forever be "looking for love [and everything else!] in all the wrong places."

So-called "tragic fate" is created when a bird attempts to be "good" by becoming a good mole because in mole circles flying is considered uncouth. It's no wonder that the moles are afraid of this winged creature; in fact, rightfully so.

In human society it is often very similar: humans prematurely condemn what they fear. Whoever does not know himself and therefore seeks a society unsuited to his nature can never be happy.

When you get to the place where you are living your own life, you have the confidence to deal with all kinds of people. You can still learn something from a bird, even if you are a mole. You do not have to become a bird to be comfortable among birds. From the start, the mole would react very differently to: "Pleased to meet you. I am a bird, but I find your life as a mole rather interesting because it is so different from my own. Tell me all about it," than he would to: "Hello, I feel so alone. Take me with you; I also want to become a good mole."

Likewise, is not a crocodile still wicked for devouring a human being, even if the person was dumb enough to swim with the crocodile in the first place?

True self-knowledge and honest self-assessment are the Alpha and Omega for a happy life. Since there are many aspects of human life, which enable or impede, we need to illuminate what we can.

The ayurvedic author, Deepak Chopra, writes that a human being thinks approximately 50,000 different thoughts a day. The result of these 50,000 thoughts—our feelings and words—generates the outer circumstances in which we live. One can actually say that the circumstances of one's life and the people that shape these circumstances mirror our inner condition.

If you doubt this, I recommend that you keep a diary of your thoughts for one week. You must list in this diary what you've been thinking about every two hours. You may do this more frequently, but I do not recommend going longer than two hours between entries because the real self-recognition effect would then become lost. After one week, read through all your thoughts. Are they compatible with the quality of your life or not?

When I examine my thoughts by means of such a diary, I am quickly surprised how much good it does me, that despite the apparent nonsense of my thought patterns, there are still sharp insights to be gleaned from the process. The connection between what I think and what I want is still far from perfect. Observing oneself, alone and so consciously, has downright therapeutic effects.

Let's presume, spoken figuratively, I want to be in Rome, but my self-image places me directly in Austria. Searching for the Alpine Pass, I am surprised that I do not find it. Then, I could, by this self-discovery through thought analysis, realize: "I am not in Austria at all! I am in Norway. No wonder, I can't find the Alps. First, I must cross the water." This has nothing to do with good or bad thoughts, but merely with natural law. I must have access to the measures necessary to move me forward.

When I imagine myself already over the Alps, I must be careful not to become so preoccupied with imagining that I forget to look for a boat. I really need a boat to cross the water. It's that simple. In order to get where I want to go, I must honestly assess where I currently am.

If I am compelled by childlike ease, I simply order an airplane to Rome and *voilà!* However, I must know, whatever I do, whether I am a mole or a bird and where my current level of self-awareness really is.

That is an interesting aspect of the Cosmic Ordering Service and perhaps a reason why it sometimes works so quickly on seemingly difficult problems—when one orders without neediness or presumption. Orders to the universe require exceptional self-knowledge. You can easily become distracted, ordering things that you don't really want at all.

By "don't really want" I mean things that don't bring any satisfaction to the soul: orders devised only with the mind, in pursuit of the so-called "good life." For example, I wanted to place increasingly imposing orders—partially to test the limits of this Cosmic Ordering Service—and so placed an order to be able to live free of charge in a castle.

There were already two offers—as I mentioned in my first book—before I determined that I was better off where I was. This order was, nevertheless, quite useful. Otherwise, I would probably have dreamed for many years about romantic, old castles. Now, I limit myself, in true contentedness, to occasional visits to castles, of only a few days duration.

Furthermore, it was an important step for me to learn to recognize the difference: whether the order is merely something my mind imagines because it is dazzled by it, or something that will bring me true joy and/or benefit.

A friend of mine is far more skillful than I in only ordering what he really wants to have. However, this was not so for many years until one day when he paid me a visit (we go for long periods of time without seeing each other) and saw firsthand the results of some of my orders. That stimulated his ambition in an extraordinary way, and he drove home to tell his girlfriend all about it. The result: six months later, he called, beaming with joy, to report that this time, he apparently had managed his order quite well. A property had been given to him, and, at the same time, his not-yet-wife had received so much money that the two of them had decided to build a house together.

When the situation with Carsten and me and my new car occurred, the two of them jumped on the bandwagon: "New car? We could really use one, too! But we must save for the construction. At best, we can put ordering to the test again. And just to make sure, we will order each of us a car although we only need one."

Well, he who orders two cars and does so with the necessary ease and freshness, receives two cars. The couple was given, at the same time, two used cars that still run very well.

What distinguishes these two successful orderers is their unrestrained ease. Furthermore, they usually only order—apart from the fact that they now have one car too many—those things that they really want.

This is in contrast to the way I sometimes go about it; however, by observing my friends and readers, I learn more all the time about when, with whom, and how this whole process works.

As a general rule, it is not disastrous if you order things and later discover you really don't want them, for in so doing, you actually accelerate self-discovery. Shooting blindly, as it were, teaches you to refine your target. You are forced to explore deeper levels to uncover what you really want.

Therefore, we have determined that, in order to lead a happy and fulfilling life, one must first know what one finds fulfilling. One must recognize what makes one thrive! Sometimes, a few false starts are necessary, until one notices that the thing once regarded as the "Ultimate" simply does not satisfy.

I had suggested in my first book that most of us only grasp the surface of our circumstances, observing—consciously—the people that surround us. However, there is more to the story. All these people and circumstances are mirrors of internal conditions and can therefore, upon reflection, bear the fruit of self-knowledge.

This is most difficult for people in the public eye, for they usually receive far more attention than the sheer force of their personality could attract. Their oversolicitous handling is engendered by glitz and glitter—not by the real human being behind it. For such people, whether pop star or spiritual guru, the mirror is twisted. Consequently, their perception of self is impaired, which, in turn, impairs their ability to build a fulfilling life.

In a smaller framework, the mirror of a manager is distorted in relation to his employees. Whenever people come together with labels, shields, and ulterior motives, the mirror becomes distorted. Over time, these distortions become ingrained in a person's self-awareness.

We must therefore be on the lookout for additional opportunities to develop self-knowledge. Oftentimes, the simplest way is the best. Namely, to pause once daily, go inward and listen: What do I want? Who am I? What makes me feel really good? What, today, made me feel truly satisfied? And what has merely satisfied the so-called lower ego?

Perhaps, now is the time to dispel a long held prejudice surrounding the ego. Many people, including myself, become frightened when they are told to dissolve their ego. "What! I should dissolve myself? Somewhere in Nirvana? I want to remain myself. I do not want to become less of who I am!"

Herein lies the misunderstanding. One becomes not less, but more. Also, one must clarify what is really meant by "lower ego." It is the part of the self which one does not want to have anyway.

No human being, upon soul-searching, can find solace in his lower ego. For example, when one uses an authoritative tone to talk nonsense, with no understanding of the topic at hand, this is the lower ego. He hides behind his words from fear of exposure.

Whoever has cast off the lower ego freely admits that he hasn't the foggiest idea about the topic being discussed, and he is immune to cutting remarks. In fact, he will probably study the slinger of those remarks with a knowing gaze that says, "Ah, you also have fears! Since you cannot be more yourself, you seek security by putting others down." No doubt this startles the other person who feels, through the gaze, recognized in his deepest fears. He bites his tongue, so as to better hide himself.

The lower ego is the part of the personality that emerges out of fear. Who would not set aside this part gladly? Who would not trade his or her ego for a life of enhancement: greater abundance and freedom?

The early stages of self-knowledge are like the *Magician's Apprentice,* uncovering the motives behind his master's deeds and beliefs. Is the thought procreated by love or fear?

"You have not discovered real truth if love does not grow from it!" This was written by Hans Kruppa in his *Book of Spells.* If you would like to enrich each day with a small, inspiring thought, this is the book for you. It contains many tiny treasures of wisdom, such as:

*Illness is one*
*symptom of a life off course.*
*It stifles the flow*
*of erroneous movement*
*because a decelerated life*
*finds its way*
*back to itself.*
*The body refuses*
*further shallowness*
*and forces the life*
*into the depths.*

Brilliant, isn't it? What a nice way to set the intention for the day's activities rather than filling one's mind with the newspaper's latest dread.

# The Truth about
# Monsters and Pussycats

Thematically, this chapter actually belongs to the one preceding, "Know Yourself." It has to do with the way that excessive or displaced fears in everyday life prevent self-realization. To illustrate this point, I would like to reproduce a short discussion between a medium and his client, during an intuitive question-and-answer session. It is not the particular case that is of interest, which begins quite trivially, but one principle that reminds me of myself—at least of how I used to think some years ago.

> *Medium:* Why did you come?
> *Visitor:* I don't know. I just thought I would come once to see what this is all about.
> *Medium:* Did you think this, or was it more of a feeling?
> *Visitor:* Yes, actually more of a feeling, now that you mention it. I had the feeling, I should come.
> *Medium:* That sounds mundane and yet is an important distinction.

How can you ever live and express your internal truth when you pay so little attention to yourself that you cannot tell whether something comes straight from the mind or from feeling? This is not insignificant; it has much meaning. Begin with the small truths!

When someone asks you if you would like a cup of tea, you often say "no," even though you really want one. You don't want to cause too much work for the other person. But it is not your truth. Let's presume that once, you would, after all, just say "yes." Then, you are asked: "What *kind* of tea would you like?" You reply: "Oh, anything is all right with me." Again, that is not your truth. If you would tune into yourself for a split second, you would know which tea you want. You think it is more polite not to be yourself, to disassociate from your feelings, to say: "It is all right with me." You do not speak your truth, and you do not appreciate the other as a host. You underestimate him, that he could be overextended by a cup of tea.

Again and again, I urge folks to speak their truth. Staring down their fears, they should reveal, here and now, their most inner and most private truths. This includes being honest about everything one desires—even that single cup of tea!

You think that your deepest truth is too dreadful to face, and therefore it ensnares you. You presume a terrible monster is in the depths of your soul. However, if you begin your quest for truth with something as simple as the tea, you will soon discover that what lives inside you is no monster, but a small pussycat. Your fear makes that small cat seem like a monster, and so, your truth concerning the tea remains hidden. You make it very complicated for yourself. You should stop this immediately! Begin to speak your truth, begin with that tea and other little things in life. The rest will take care of itself. . . .

Think on it, your paramount desire. It must be completely recognized so that it can find the best path to total fulfillment.

When one has not yet found his light, he deludes himself that the task will be fraught with difficulty. Hardly does he come upon it, however, when he determines that the very form of responsibility he had feared is precisely the truth for which he had hoped.

*Our deepest fear is not that we are inadequate.*
*Our deepest fear is that we are powerful beyond measure.*
*Our light, not our darkness, frightens us most.*

—Marianne Williamson

# How Does the Cosmic Ordering Service Work?

Many people have already recognized that their outside reality is largely determined by the character and quality of their thoughts and feelings. In extreme cases, the interior is equal to the exterior, and the life circumstances that a person creates are in direct response to how he thinks and feels.

Some strive to master recurring internal darkness by difficult exercises, or they attempt to force only positive thoughts. That may work for some people, but for me it was too much work. Also, I could not get into daily affirmations and visualizations, although I know many folks who swear by this approach. Whatever works. The measure of the effectiveness is the measure of the truth. I do not find that any of this contradicts my technique. One can try a different technique with each wish and remain with the one that proves the most effective.

Through coincidental experiences, I have determined that a single clear thought, sent to the universe with full intent is sufficient to drown out internal chaos. This pure thought actualizes itself again and again with amazing precision. It is the abbreviated form of positive thinking!

An order with the universe works essentially the same way as a physical order with an arbitrary mail-order firm. The only difference is that, when dealing with the universe, one neither calls, faxes, nor e-mails. An order with the universe is much simpler. One imagines the order, sending it forth in thought. Or one writes it down or expresses it aloud. The vehicle used is of no consequence. What matters is the crystallization of one's desire. For example: "Hello, Universe! I order a new job, a new house, a blue velvet dress, an optimal vacation spot with nice people at the resort"—or, or, or . . . fill in the blank with whatever you truly desire.

The universe will accommodate whatever little rituals *you* need to increase your faith in the process (after all, the universe knows you inside and out; it understands that you need these reassurances). It can create an environment conducive to the feeling of an order "well sent." And this feeling will ensure that it is so. For example, let's say you prefer to write down your order and preserve the note in a special place. You could do this at night because, by looking at the stars, you have a better sense of the vast magnificence of the universe. If you like, you may even set up candles to increase your sense of connection to the elements.

If you require a lot of fuss, you could even jot down your order on a piece of wax paper and toss it into the sugar bowl. Whatever you do, make it fun.

Many people obtain good results standing on their balcony, beneath the starlit sky; however, I have been quite successful placing orders while sitting on the toilet . . . there are no rules.

Likewise no rules, but useful advice: always order with the unaffectedness of a child and with the belief that the order has already been fulfilled. Then, forget about it. There is basic logic behind this. You wouldn't order bathroom supplies from a company that you presumed to be too stupid to process your order, would you?

Since you place orders only with companies that you trust to deliver, you do not place an order and then call them to confirm that they understood what a towel or a bar of soap is or whether they need you to explain it to them. If you behaved in such a manner, you would probably be flagged as a problem customer with that company. Well, the same applies to the universe. If you check and recheck, redefine or reorder, the universe—like any distributor—presumes that you are somewhat confused in the head or, at least, unsure of what you want. In such a case, it presumes—and rightly so—that it is probably best not to send you anything at all.

Affirmations are fundamentally a different technique, which have nothing to do with cosmic orders. With affirmations, one repeats—again and again—the same thing. If this kind of slow, lulling of the spirit works for you, great! You can also give the Cosmic Ordering Service a try. They are not mutually exclusive.

# What I Think
## Creates What I Experience

There is much evidence that the sum of all our thoughts, feelings, and words produces the outside circumstances in which we live. Turned around, our life circumstances reflect our mental state, just as the people we attract reflect our internal condition. Presented as a hypothesis: your thoughts create your reality, whether directly or indirectly.

How many of your thoughts, which you noted during the last week, would be suitable for creating the life you want?

For me, the relationship is often disastrous—I admit it! After I had kept the aforementioned thought diary for one week, parts of it made me wonder how I had managed to remain alive at all! My thought-hygiene, if you will, leaves a lot to be desired. My intentions to think constructively are apparently not enough. As Goethe wrote: "It is not enough to know, one must also apply it. It is not sufficient to want, one must also do."

As my thought diary revealed to me, I, unfortunately, do not put all my resolutions and everything that I know into practice. Behind this, an important message is hidden: it seems to be completely sufficient for one to be a "work in progress." One need not be perfect for this to work!

Whoever comes to the realization that he is as good as he can be at the moment has done enough to be supported, seemingly led by magic hands. This as-good-as-I-can-be-at-the-moment man might not seem like much from the outside, yet he is, nonetheless, capable of creation.

There are people who give the impression of a bull in a china shop. In other words, they possess little insight and mow others down like a steam roller. That may be our impression. Nevertheless, these impossible creatures seem to receive divine aid, and we look on with astonishment: "Universe, what is this about? What do you think you are doing? How can you support jerks like these? And what about me? I am so good and nice and moral. When do you support me in such a way? This is so unfair! You should be fair. If not you, then who?"

If we were able to understand the signs of the universe, then a possible response could be: "Here speaks the universe, the Cosmic Ordering Service, the All-Oneness, or if you like, just call me Joe! You want to know why I support these humans, whom you regard as useless 'jerks.' Carelessly expressed, they admittedly, now and then, wreak havoc. However, they also have difficult personalities. In the middle of their havoc, it often dawns on them that they have pushed others too far. At that point, they truly strive to make amends immediately."

"Oh," you could then object. "I haven't seen any evidence of that. This good-for-nothing has never apologized to me."

"You are right; it would have been nice if he had occasionally done that. Nevertheless, you shouldn't judge so harshly. Please consider, those with psychological complexes and weak characters can be extremely afraid to admit even the smallest mistake. It is difficult for them to apologize. However, this 'jerk' feels honest regret over his behavior. And he does—often anonymously—rectify many of his errors. He may have other good qualities, for example, perhaps he is forgiving and would, in an emergency, come to the aid of even his greatest adversary. This means that he, admittedly, has not yet evolved enough to know better. However, within the context of his given consciousness, he makes considerable effort to do the best he can. And in these moments of his greatest effort, I will support him again and again. His inner wisdom is already interested in finding a fulfilling life; therefore, he receives, for each second of honest joy in living, some small miracle as a reward.

"Furthermore, you should consider that human beings do not only communicate through words but also through subliminal thoughts and feelings that are often contradictory without one being aware of it. This communication is inevitable. From the outside, you can never really determine what is going on inside another. Therefore, you should not rashly condemn the behavior or way of life of others. It is your task to recognize your own way. With this, you should be fully occupied." Thus (possibly) spoke "Joe."

The idea that communication also consists of subliminal thoughts and feelings takes me back to the first time I encountered "reverse speech" nearly a year ago. Reverse speech belongs to those things that reveal the ingenious variety and wondrous interweaving of life.

If one records normal conversation and then plays it backward on a tape recorder, an experienced therapist can hear in this gibberish, every thirty seconds or so, sentences and words which sound like normal speech. These so-called reversals reveal—beyond what he has stated—what the speaker actually thinks and feels. It is a method for uncovering whether or not one is in harmony with his or her inherent nature. If so, then the reverse speech and everyday forward speech are attuned. If not, one can receive, from this technology, illuminating insights. Above all, one cannot contradict them, since one really said these things—even if "backwards."

In the United States, reverse speech has become a recognized form of therapy. The discoverer, David Oates, even used it once with a murderer, who for a full hour had vehemently protested his innocence. Backwards, however, he not only confessed to the murder, but also revealed his motive and the hiding place of the weapon.

The police followed this lead and found, at the indicated place, the weapon with the fingerprints of the accused, who still protested his innocence.

In Germany, there are entire institutes devoted to *Rückwärtssprache* (the German term for reverse speech). (See recommended resources for more information.)

I am addressing this subject simply to illustrate how much interaction really occurs between two humans as they converse, and just how far, both energetically and essentially, this exchange in normal language can be from the truth. The good Joe's advice, therefore, that we "should not rashly condemn" is valuable indeed.

Also, his reference to "honest joy in living" for which there would be "some small miracle as a reward," reminds me of the story of a man, who had a near-death experience and then wrote a book about it (unfortunately, both the author and the title escape me). The man died, experiencing what had already become a recognized phenomenon: sliding through a long, dark tunnel toward the light. As his entire life flashed before him, all the negative experiences came forward in his mind's eye and were deleted, one by one, from his memory. However, those of a positive nature were stored for "positive karma."

What astonished the man most was which events were deleted as "negative" and which were classified as "well done." Situations in which he had acted morally, in his opinion, had not left him with a good feeling. He had acted out of a sense of obligation and had felt badly anyway. Such experiences showed up as negative and were deleted.

In other cases, it was the complete opposite. There were situations in which he had violated, or so he thought, moral and social standards, yet all involved had experienced joy. Little to no morality, but joy in living for all. These experiences were already stored as positive—and with commendation, at that! The man was happily bemused. Obviously, the yardstick was not the social standard or the alleged morality, but the joy-quotient of those involved. How much differently would he have run his life if only he could have known that before!

Since his soul decided to return to life with this new realization, the resuscitation efforts of the doctors were successful, and he was able to report his experiences to the world via his book. Thus, "honest joy in living" resulted in "some small miracle as a reward."

Incidentally, I can confirm Joe's suggestion that the way people seem on the outside oftentimes does not reflect their inner workings.

For example, in the case of autism, it is easy to presume—based on their behavior—that these folks have the intellect of an insect. Birger Sellin, who is autistic, completely dispelled this prejudice, one day, when someone gave him a computer. Since then, he writes books and obviously has a strong grasp of language. This, despite the fact that everyone around him thought he couldn't even count to three.

It is indeed true that everyone has more than enough to do to investigate his own interior. If you can honestly face yourself and, within the context of your present realizations, make the effort to lead a happy and fulfilling life, then you will certainly receive complete support from the universe or "Joe."

If you do something stupid from which nothing better develops (at least, not yet), you shouldn't worry. As long as you are growing in self-awareness, observing your thoughts, taking it all in stride, you will—slowly but surely—through conscious thoughts and feelings create the reality in which you truly wish to live. As long as you remain committed to this ever-evolving journey, you will receive "magical" support.

Should you, again, in mid-trek fall completely "asleep" (as I often do) the alarm clock will sound—at first, quite discreetly. You will notice that life has become more arduous because your divine providences have diminished. No longer will those things you need be placed, at exactly the right time, directly at your feet. For example, the rapid-transit railway is suddenly late, and you must wait eighteen minutes, instead of seeing the train emerge just as you step onto the platform.

I directly became acquainted with this concept by missing a series of trains at a low point in my consciousness. In supported reality this simply does not happen. The rapid-transit railway is a simple, but symbolic example—like everything else in life.

For two days, I had been stuck in a discontented and edgy state; furthermore, I was not consciously aware of my gloominess. Therefore, the "alarm clock" rang: the rapid-transit railway drove off four minutes too early in the freezing cold, and I had to wait fifteen minutes. On the return trip, the same thing happened. Since, in such things, I am somewhat pampered, thanks to the Cosmic Ordering Service, I became readily suspicious.

When I, once again, had to wait on the following day, I knew something simply wasn't right. I stopped to grouse and grumble, searched my consciousness for a solution, and became attuned to the situation. The next day, I wanted— with renewed energy—to arrive extra early at a customer's, with whom I was trying to reestablish a relationship. (I work, among other things, as a graphic designer). However, I foolishly neglected to set the alarm clock and so overslept by exactly one hour. "Why did I mess up now, again, of all times?" I wondered. "Why couldn't everything just as easily have gone the other way?"

Soon, it became clear to me, what was going on, as I sat in the rapid-transit railway and heard the driver say that we would be delayed due to an accident. As it turned out, railway traffic on my route was completely blocked for over one hour, and the train, in which I sat, was positioned first and could therefore drive through again on a clear track with only a ten minute delay. I drew a deep breath. Obviously, everything had been as it should be. The universe had saved me one hour of waiting in control rooms of the rapid-transit railway. The ringing of the alarm—or, in this case, the lack thereof—had allowed me to sleep in instead. "Thank you, Universe, for this small success!" Since then, the rapid-transit railway always comes the moment I appear at the platform.

The same will, no doubt, happen for you as you clean up your thought-hygiene. There is no reason, however, for you to make more effort than is enjoyable for you. Everything is always granted with tranquility. The motivations will reveal themselves, in the external, more clearly, over time. If your internal condition becomes more recognizable in a smoothly functioning outside reality, then it will become that much more fun for you to play around with it until everything in your life flows easily.

## Don't Count Your Chickens before They Are Hatched

In my first book, I now realize that I neglected to sufficiently stress one small, but important detail. It concerns the doubts, which erase all orders, and the closely connected fact that you should in no case "count your chickens before they are hatched."

For one thing, doubts destroy the energy required to manifest orders into reality; not because the Cosmic Ordering Service refuses to deliver, but rather, because you stubbornly refuse to accept.

I have had my share of problems with "delivery acceptance." Once, I had placed a certain order, whose delivery I both wanted to accept and yet could not. Eventually, information and allusions concerning a particular organization kept popping up again and again. This, however, left me completely cold. Again and again, this organization's meetings were brought to my attention, and each time I thought: "Yikes! What is this? In any case, it is nothing for me!"

After I had heard, read, or been told about this organization for, at least, the fiftieth time, I decided to give it a try—just once. I also like surprises and unusual experiences, and so I went to a meeting because I regarded it as a kind of amusement. Once there, however, I found a direct connection to what I had ordered so long ago. It was clearly a case of persistent delivery non-acceptance. I could have received the order much sooner.

The more you remain in a state of doubt, the less relaxed you become and therefore the less receptive. You simply do not catch on when the universe drops hints concerning where you can pick up your order. Unfortunately, it can even ring the doorbell, and you may not even bother to open the door.

Nonetheless, you will have ample opportunity to encounter these hints of the delivery in everyday life, provided you follow—to any degree—your true life path. In some cases (like mine) you can even stumble around blindly for months and still eventually end up with a fulfilled order. Sometimes, though, it is possible to miss a delivery once and for all, if you have thwarted many delivery attempts.

Such self-imposed blockades, which obstruct the flow of goodness, develop often, when one proclaims his order to everyone before it has been delivered. Remember that each clear and organized thought, which is released and arrives free of anxiety, returns to the sender like a boomerang, manifesting in the physical.

Let's presume, you now tell everyone: "I have now ordered a new car for myself from the universe. However, I haven't a penny to my name. From the surplus of the universe, I will obtain this car." It is as if one becomes the thought-boomerang, catapulted into the universe not from spiritual power but as one who manages the order, placing it on a shelf for all to see. This thought has serious manifestation problems.

One can also introduce oneself as a seed, which grows up in the soil of the spirit to become a plant (the manifestation). If I excavate the seed from the spirit and show it everywhere, then the fertile soil needed for growth is missing. It is far more meaningful to leave the seeds in the soil (in the spirit) and then, when all admire the mature plant, it will be apparent which seed (i.e. thought) was the father or the mother of this manifestation.

To put it out to the universe means to suspend all doubts of both yourself and your fellow man. One certainly comes into an obligation with: "I have already told everyone that I ordered a car. It is about time for it to come. How do I show my face otherwise? Already, the ill-meaning questions are pouring in." And so, one feels under pressure and stress. Thus the spirit loses its ease and power, and one cannot release the order.

If I do not release the boomerang, it cannot return. Even if the universe should grant a "beginner credit" and overlook the incorrect filling out of the purchase order, preparing for a special distribution, it would still be received questionably—even in the unlikely event that one is still relaxed enough to be at the right place at the right time, for the order to be received. Thus, there are many reasons to hold your tongue, reporting your order only after achieving success.

In my case, this problem dissolved semi-automatically. In 1996, I appeared on two talk shows to discuss ordering with the universe, as well as my book on coincidences (still in manuscript form). I imagined that, from this, many people would report amazing coincidences that they had experienced, which I could soak up for the book I was writing at the time.

In fact, coincidences seem to be hardly a topic at all, as it is clear to nearly everyone that there are no "coincidental" coincidences, but rather, possibilities that one creates or attracts (thus the coincidence book became superfluous).

After the second show aired, I received many letters from viewers. However, no one wanted to report a coincidence. More than half wrote something like this: "How interesting! Where can I get a catalog for this mail-order house, *Universe?* They seem to have everything! I would be very much obliged if you could send me the telephone number and price list. . . ."

I could hardly believe it. Did I express myself so indistinctly? Motivated by a burning desire to dispel this ignorance and to enlighten folks on how to truly access this "mail-order house," I sat down and wrote—in three days—the first book in this series, *The Cosmic Ordering Service.*

Then, I copied the manuscript and sold it to all who were interested. In this way, I placed several hundred copies in the public eye until Omega-Verlag made a wonderful little book from it.

After I sold the first hundred copies, a problem began to present itself. An increasing number of people called me: some of them to enthusiastically report all the wonderful orders that had already been delivered, still others, to inquire why for them it simply didn't work. Interestingly, those with successful orders to report were—based on their telephone voice—open, happy, and relaxed people, while those with less satisfactory results sounded sad, tense, and demanding.

However, most callers had one thing in common: they regarded me as a kind of "Master" in the utilization of the Cosmic Ordering Service. Surely, I succeed immediately with whatever I order! Well, all one needs to do is read chapter 2 of this book, in which I describe the dread of facing a hefty payment of back taxes, thanks to an unconscious order. This was not masterly by any stretch. Fortunately, one can continually fine-tune an order and thus solve the problem.

These high expectations of my readers, including the readers of my magazine, *Solar Wind*, fed into my desire to succeed. In addition, I already had the same problem as so many others: I had spoken of my order before the universe had a chance to deliver.

I felt bad because I had ordered a castle and then found out that I didn't really want to live in a castle at all—not even free of charge. It turned out that my independence within my own four walls pleased me even more. Since I had announced to everyone, however, that I had ordered up a castle, people asked me repeatedly: "So, when are you going to move into one of these castles?" And I thought: "Leave me alone, already, about castles! They, with their dark, archaic energy. And who will clean all those rooms? Certainly not I!"

The upshot: I felt pressured by the expectations of both my readers and those of my social circle. The chain of improbable compliance and unbelievable coincidences had been broken—fortunately not completely—but orders of really large things, such as castles, would simply no longer work. The entire process, then, had culminated in this huge, false order, which luckily, with the help of a friend, could be corrected.

Since then, I hold fast to this policy: if someone asks me precisely what I have ordered, I reply: "Why, I already have everything. I didn't order anything in particular, just one lovely surprise each day—and thus it comes." That is pretty harmless, closing the door on potential stress.

# Where There Is a Problem, There Is Also a Solution

Concerning problems, I have a motto: wherever one appears, a solution cannot be far. A problem without a solution can no more exist than a medal with only one side. It would cease to be a medal. It would not exist and with it also the other side, namely the problem, could not. The existence of a problem, therefore, proves to me that there must be a solution to it somewhere.

Now, there are problems whose solutions could lie somewhat farther away than I would like, at the moment. However, I am of the opinion that there must always be a temporary solution, which is good enough to make me perfectly happy in the here and now.

When the orders only work at half strength, what then can I do to receive everything I would like, including all absurdities?

Do I hear any voices that call me greedy? Be glad that I am greedy enough to always want the best in life; otherwise, how could I teach you how to achieve it?

I think, one of the reasons many people read my magazine—or for that matter, my latest book—is that I, myself, am unholy and unenlightened, and yet, I'm allowed to receive many amusements and conveniences from the Cosmic Ordering Service. The underlying message for you: "Well, if this crazy lady can create so much abundance, then I certainly can, too!"

That brings me to a fitting topic—particularly important for beginners in circles of mystics and psychics who have had experiences with the incomprehensible. If, at first, one is astonished or baffled by such experiences, one would usually like to know more about how to use them. What does one do? One attends seminars, workshops, and lectures of all kinds. So far, so good. Yet, not much is truly learned. Nonetheless, one does become acquainted with like-minded individuals and thus becomes more inspired. But one must not forget: just because a person recognizes that there are mental laws and invisible forces, does not necessarily mean he is a good person! He may have determined simply through intelligence and experience: "Aha, the spirit controls the material! And anyone with mastery over his own thoughts can control those with thoughts in chaos." Even more interesting: "Over whom could I practice this power? Where are the stupid ones that I could exploit?"

There are such people in the so-called New Age scene, just as there are evolved, loving, and kind-hearted beings as well. You should not follow the first guru you encounter and let him make decisions for you. Only by listening to your inner voice can you determine your truth. No one can ever be a better advisor than your own inner authority. Although those around you may sometimes tune in to the tender calls of your inner voice before you do, you are the only one who can separate what is true from what is not.

How do you figure this out? Quite simply: you have not found truth if love has not increased! In other words, you only need to follow your sense of well-being. If Mr. Guru tells you that your problem is this or that and, upon hearing this, you feel more open, more at peace, or in any way more positive than before, then the guru uncovered at least some of the truth and is certainly not all bad. However, if you say to yourself: "Yes, this sounds logical enough. He is probably right," yet you feel worse than before, Mr. Guru is probably selling nonsense. Enough! Get as far away as possible!

It really is time to stop idolizing gurus. Those who do not acknowledge their own gurus, within, will never find fulfillment. It is fine to allow an "outside guru" to inspire you. If his presence causes you to feel better about yourself, or he is able to dissipate tension from parts of your body that you didn't even know were tense, then you have found someone who—at least, for today—is a source of spiritual energy for you. That does not mean, however, that he is a better human than you are, or that, tomorrow, he will continue to be good for you, or that you would not receive even greater help from your own internal wisdom.

The more positive your thoughts and feelings, the more positive your life becomes (provided you are being honest with yourself and not hiding negative thoughts behind positive affirmations). My success stress, which developed because I am allegedly the Master Orderer, was a problem. There had to be a solution.

When I have a problem, for which no solution comes easily to mind, I take a short respite for silent meditation, looking deeply inside myself for an answer. In this instance, no matter how much I considered it, I couldn't figure it out. Formerly, in such cases, I have ordered the answer for anytime in the near future. Then, in the course of the next few days, someone said something illuminating to me, relevant to the topic at hand, or I read something that resonated, or I simply sensed the answer.

Regarding my current dilemma with success, my internal voice at last revealed that no matter how cleverly I write about it, my readers can never manifest quite as easily. It is not simply a question of modeling the success of another. Unfortunately, one usually orders unconsciously. Nonetheless, the sum of all thoughts and feelings constantly comes to us, in the same way, as unconscious orders. The physical manifestation mirrors what one really thinks and feels.

My thought diary brought to light the fact that I belonged to a group of people that fed off one another's confusion. If I continued to block my orders with an anxious expectation of success, then I had only one choice: I must purge all undesirable automatism. If I could remain in a state of deliberate consciousness, I could control my thoughts, directing their energies to create only positive outcomes. Then, I could preserve for myself the individualized, targeted orders, and there would be no more unwanted, unconscious manifestations!

Yeah, right. Anyone with a mindset similar to mine, who had gained self-awareness by use of a thought diary, would from such a suggestion either become powerless from fear or would just resort to a joke to lighten up the intensity. Such a suggestion cannot be true: all thoughts and feelings clarified, cleansed by virtue of conscious selection!

That would mean no more memory reruns to assuage boredom; no more daydreams, whose content is nurtured from old thought patterns; no abstract observations of other people's shortcomings; no more sullen and annoying thoughts; no more value judgments; no more fear or fury, melancholia, or aggression; no more twisted pleasures from plotting the punishment of those one perceives to be "in the wrong."

Now, it is true that I, as soon as I become aware of such a dark thought—sometimes immediately, sometimes as much as an hour later—decide: "Okay, you have wallowed in your vengeful thinking long enough. Now, try to see it from the other person's perspective, finding a solution that allows you both to emerge victorious, instead of proving how right you are."

I suspect it is this tendency in both my thoughts and intentions that creates my so-called good luck. I am, at last, operating in accordance with my level of realization and thus endeavor to make the most of any situation.

However, what this inner voice had proposed to me—to eliminate all unconscious and automatic thinking—was probably somewhat exaggerated and not meant to be taken literally. After all, the beauty of the Cosmic Ordering Service is that one can be unholy, completely devoid of solemn seriousness, and still reap the benefits. So far, there had been no reason for me to behave like a saint. An occasional organized thought had proved to be sufficient. And now this. Disastrous! Besides, the whole thing sounded like way too much effort. I love my comfort and intend to maintain it.

This led me to an idea: "This universe with its exaggerated efforts! I will throw a monkey wrench into its holy ideas." I then came up with a new order: "Okay, dear Universe, I can see that by publishing my experiences, I have done myself a dubious service because as a result I have since felt under scrutiny. As I can never order anything except what the synergy of my thoughts and feelings creates, it is obvious that I must do something about my thoughts and feelings. I therefore order that you invent a simple method, with which I can clean and arrange my thoughts easily and effortlessly. If that is simply not possible, then I suggest a new order, that everything I want, I continue to receive. Thank you in advance for the sympathetic treatment."

I considered myself to be quite clever and so expected an intuition of how I could turn off the doubts and become unaffected by the pressure to succeed, so that the orders could function in their proven way with bigger things.

Not much later, however, I found myself facing the realization that life doesn't tolerate stagnancy, and it expected me to eventually bring *all* my thoughts and feelings into conscious orders. For the moment, I should probably begin by at least improving the percentage of my conscious thoughts to place me, somewhat, on the path. Good gracious!

Regarding the unsuccessful positive thinkers: they are the ones that, out of principle, murmur: "All goes well for me, all goes well," while, underneath the surface, they feel that all goes miserably and nothing can help them. If these unsuccessful positive thinkers had the deep conviction twenty-four hours a day that their thoughts create reality, then whatever ulterior motive lay behind "nothing good comes; all goes badly for me" would lose its appeal. Thus, the spirit would arrive at the desired effect.

"Recognize yourself and the power of your spirit, the instigator of all your outside circumstances!" In order to really do that, one must devise something of a system to combat counterproductive thoughts.

By the way, what one avoids, one internalizes. Therefore, do not shy away from your negative thoughts.

Acknowledge them; say "thank you" to them, for they are a necessary bump in the road, along your path to self-discovery.

As the saying goes, "Those who can, do; those who can't, teach!" Therefore, you might think I am not fully illuminated, since I write books and articles supposedly to teach you "how." Yet, I am inspired by you as much as you are from me. This is a collective process. We are helping each other to grow, day by day. Remember that enlightenment does not need us to exist.

## The Enlightenment Doesn't Care How You Attained It

As with most things in life, when using the Cosmic Ordering Service, you don't necessarily receive the direct fulfillment of your wishes, but rather, the outcome of your beliefs. You can outsmart yourself by drowning out your disorganized, somber, automatic, everyday thoughts with positive, facile, lucid ideas, sending forth quasi orders.

If the orders are successfully released, even by rote, they will achieve manifestation, as long as you do not send forth any doubts after the fact. So that you don't do this mindlessly, you should start with simple things, and then reinforce your belief on the basis of previous successes. Everything you believe, you manifest.

Therefore, it is most important to free yourself from as much fear, doubt, worry, and damaging dogma as possible. How you achieve this is of no consequence.

*The Enlightenment Doesn't Care How You Attained It* is the apt title for an inspiring little book by Thaddeus Golas. And so it is. Likewise, you shouldn't worry about the methods you use to attain the enlightenment. Simply put: discover what works for you; then just do it.

For example, some folks keep a journal of their wishes, writing them down every evening. This would seem, to me, like an imposition; however, for them, the "imposition" is a good thing, creating the sense of serious commitment their psyche obviously requires. Well, great! More power to them. Most importantly, it works!

The purpose of my writing is not to instigate new dogmas, stipulating "you must do this and this." First and foremost, I write because it's fun . . . and now you have to pay the price. All kidding aside, I hope that this book inspires you to effect change in your life.

You may smile and say to yourself: "Now, all I need to do is create a mental picture of something that would please me and learn how to convince my subconscious to believe in what I wish. If Barbel's crazy methods work, then mine certainly will!"

If you think like this, you are on the sure path to success. It truly does not matter if you do what I propose, or the exact opposite, or even something completely different. Here, I am simply sharing with you a few success stories, along with some mistakes and misunderstandings. If this encourages you to proceed along your own path, then perhaps I will receive a letter from you about all your successful orders. That will make me very happy.

Here's a story that did just that. Even before the first edition of *The Cosmic Ordering Service* was released, my publisher had given the manuscript to a friend who had little patience with "all this esoteric crap." Nonetheless, he found my little book sufficiently intriguing to try placing at least one order with the universe. So, as a test, he ordered a new girlfriend. Since he really didn't believe in "such nonsense," he forgot all about the order. (The best thing he could have done!) Barely two weeks later, he met a new friend. He enthusiastically called the publishing house to report his success.

Shortly after my book had been published, he and his new girlfriend were married. Since they both firmly believed that they had met thanks to the order with the universe, they gave all their wedding guests a copy of the book, so that they too could order something beautiful.

This orderer had luck on his side in that he did not take himself too seriously, forgetting about his order immediately. He did not dwell on it enough to allow any doubts to arise; therefore, the order was free to attract the necessary positive energy for its manifestation.

Some clever folks use visualization to overlay their negative notions with images of positive outcomes to banish persistent doubts. This is not for lazy people, like me. It can work; however one must observe oneself honestly. Who can say, perhaps by focusing so much energy on my mind's eye, I might only nurture my doubts even more?

You must decide for yourself what works best for you. You must explore the depths of yourself to determine what you truly think and feel while exploring this or that technique.

If you rejoice inside because you quietly sent an order to the universe without telling a soul, then that is right for you. If it calms, strengthens, and pleases you to compose your orders in the evening as beautiful essays, then that, simply, is right for you. However, by no means, will you get around the fact that you must, in order to thrive, not only find, but recognize, yourself.

Recognizing your true self is not at all difficult. On the contrary, you use much more energy trying to hide from yourself which is like using every possible trick to remain in the shadows of a well-lit stage. That takes strength.

Furthermore, if one attempts to block out the world by squeezing one's eyes shut, only distorted images will result. It is hard to believe how many people are afraid of what lies dormant within them. They believe the darkness will some-how become darker if they shine the light of awareness upon it. And the more aware they become, the darker are the sacks they pull over their heads.

Concerning this subject, it would be difficult to top the words of Marianne Williamson, quoted in chapter 4. ("Our deepest fear is not that we are inadequate. Our deepest fear is that we are powerful beyond measure. Our light, not our darkness, frightens us most.") The best one can do is add clarity by the use of vivid examples: whoever looks into the heavens to find the universe sees only clouds if he does not look deeply enough. The clouds are not the universe. Equally so with human beings. The clouds are not the human soul. One should therefore remove all clouds—i.e., sacks over the head—to free up the view.

Whoever recognizes his true being can easily identify the right path for himself. I therefore propose that you take out a piece of paper and write down your beliefs, surround-ing what you would like to have.

Here are a couple of examples of what may appear on your paper:


• Without belief, nothing meaningful comes.

Therefore, I will never have anything meaningful if
I don't believe it is possible.

• Fears are never meaningful; they only prove that
I believe something outside myself controls my
reality.

You could also add to your list why you find it meaningful to believe the opposite of what you desire in your life.
Obviously, you decide again and again to do just that; otherwise, you would already have everything you wished. Why
do you do this?

Here's what I wrote: "I would not like to be disappointed in the event that it doesn't work out; therefore, I
believe the worst." However, I realized right away that "first,
I must see it, then, I will believe it" simply does not work.
The universe's response to that is always: "As soon as you
believe it, you will see it done."

Another popular dogma is: "I could become too lazy if I
am firmly convinced that I can have everything I want."
Upon further reflection, this is total humbug. The anticipa-
tion of good things actually creates more energy, therefore
making one even more active.

These are just a few small examples. Everyone has
his/her own crazy reasons for self-sabotage. Just remember to
recognize yourself, and then, believe in what you wish for.
(La-la-la. Cling-bing. OM. That is just beautiful relaxation
music to help you write your list . . .)

# How Do I Succeed in Having a Problem?

You read correctly. It does say: how do I succeed in having a problem? I did not forget to add the negative. Most of us were brought up to believe that problems are a normal occurrence. Now, imagine, hypothetically, that you meet someone from another world, where problems do not exist. How do you explain the concept to him or her? It would not be easy. If the nature of the other world truly has no framework, then it would seem to them that the generation of problems in itself would be an art.

The fairytale woman, *Mary*, from the novel of the same name by Ella Kensington (formerly Bodo and Gina Deletz) comes from such a world. In this netherworld, Mary comes upon a new game that she finds especially funny. The game is called "we have a problem."

"Umm," she thinks, "this sounds pretty funny and downright crazy! In any case, I also want to learn how to have a problem. What fun!"

Mary's wish to visit the Earth is granted, and she immediately assumes human form. She then begins her quest to find a problem. With an envious gaze, she studies everyone that claims to have a problem. However, Mary, herself, has only one dilemma: she simply does not understand how anyone has a problem.

The more she questions the "fortunate ones," who possess such a desirable commodity, the bleaker it appears for Mary because their problems dissolve in the conversation with her. Therefore, she learns nothing.

The situation seems to improve when Michael, a man burdened by his problems, falls in love with her. Nonetheless, it ends tragically, for Michael learns how to eliminate his problems!

Likewise, it could go this way for any reader of *Mary*, since many problems in life are relative: the situation, itself, is not the problem, but what one thinks about it.

Two people can be at the same place at the same time. One of them can be completely happy, while the other is miserable. The realization of this alone can eliminate many problems by encouraging one to stop allowing those little happy moments in life to pass by, wasted.

A real-life example of this is the former editor-in-chief of the French magazine, *Elle,* Jean-Dominique Bauby, who suffered a stroke at the age of forty-three. Afterwards, he found himself cleansed in spirit, in a body that was paralyzed completely. He could not even swallow. Scarcely could he move anything except his left eyelid. Nonetheless, with what few faculties remained, Bauby managed the unfathomable: he dictated a book about his new life, mostly implied through the movements of his own body, of which he was now a prisoner.

To read his book, *The Butterfly and the Diving Bell,* is to be confronted with the reality of not truly discovering one's life until it is already past. One is mercilessly reminded that some so-called problems are nothing less than missed opportunities for "those little happy moments."

In the creation of Bauby's book, the letters of the French alphabet were written in the order of their frequency and recited again and again. If the correct letter was hit upon, J.D. twitched his eyelid. His patient helper, Claude Mendibil, completed the entire book with him in this way.

Bauby dictated the last day of his normal life. After awakening, sullenly and carelessly, beside his beautiful wife, he had hastily taken care of all the then tiresome chores like shaving, showering, and breakfasting. All of that ordinariness now seemed to him like a true miracle. "Today, it seems to me that my whole life will have been one long chain of such small failures and missed chances," he dictated.

Bauby passed away September 3, 1997, leaving a book that both sorrowfully and humorously asks each reader: "And what about those fleeting little happy moments of chance in your life? Are they a chain of small failures and missed opportunities or is your soul content, with no need to resort to a 'thunderclap' to startle you into conscious living?"

Jean-Dominique concluded his book with the words: "Is there a key in this cosmos to unlatch my diving bell? A train without a final stop? A currency strong enough to buy back my freedom? I must search elsewhere. I make my own way."

Maybe it is a radical cure, but nevertheless not a bad idea, to assess some of the problems one encounters on a daily basis against the benchmark "how would someone like Jean-Dominique Bauby have viewed this situation after his stroke?"

Now, I am not being as banal as: "There are people much worse off than you; therefore, you should be content . . ." Rather, I am saying: look at your life consciously, asking yourself, honestly, what are the real problems? Also: are you taking advantage of every opportunity to bring luck and joy into your life? If you don't seek out these opportunities, how else will they come your way?

The mythical figure of Mary approaches the problem-free state in quite a different—and much more humorous—manner.

People are individuals and therefore very different in the way they process information; however, let's now have some fun with this whole problem thing. Forgive me for taking liberties with the two authors' work.

A favorite chapter of mine is where Mary is mistakenly transported to a mental hospital, where she simply cannot find out who are the sick and who are the staff. However, she finally figures it out: the sick persons must be the ones in white because most of them are so tense and grumpy—poor things!

However, I do not want to spoil your enjoyment: please read it for yourself, so that you may catch whatever pertains to you personally.

Mary's spirit guide reveals to her that it is not easy to remain unhappy. One would need to do many complicated things for this to occur. If one does not pause to think, then he or she would be automatically happy. The unhappy person must, therefore, work at it.

Mary tries to approach the matter step-by-step, interviewing all the unhappy people that she can find. One example was a secretary in a big company. Mary discovers that this woman is unhappy because she feels small and powerless. Mary would like to learn more about this, and so she sits next to this secretary in the lunchroom, asking naïvely:

"Why do you make yourself feel so small?"

"How do you mean that, Ms. Mary?" asks the secretary in amazement.

"I think your boss has the feeling that he is more important than you, and you, in turn, feel worthless. But how, exactly, do you create this feeling—that you are inferior to your boss?"

"Your point is well taken, Ms. Mary. I will put a stop to it right now. No longer will I allow him to treat me like his property. I thank you! Thank you!"

"Has everything been turned upside down?" Mary wondered. "I ask completely normal questions and never get a straight answer. Instead, all I receive is gratitude for inspiration I don't even know I am giving."

It continues in this way for the "unfortunate" Mary. The more she drills the others to find out how they create their problems, the less she understands. The answers she receives simply do not seem sensible to her. However, she refuses to give up. Encountering a woman who appears to be extremely unhappy, Mary's hopes are restored. Perhaps she will find out more this time.

"Susanne, would you please enlighten me? How do you manage to be so unhappy?"

"Are you asking what makes me unhappy?"

"Actually, it would interest me much more to know how exactly you make yourself so unhappy."

"I don't understand what you mean. I don't create my problems myself!"

"Who then creates them, if it is not you?" Mary asks in puzzlement.

Mary, in a dream, returns to her spirit guide, asking why Susanne could not understand that she, herself, was creating her problems.

Mary's spirit guide—called Ella—patiently explains: "If people fully understood that their problems were of their own making, they would only become guilty—not a good thing for them. Therefore, they have forgotten that they, themselves, create the problems.

Furthermore, this act of forgetting is an important component of the Earth game, in order to be able to create problems continuously. If you take full responsibility for your problems, it is easy to get rid of them. However, if you assign the blame to something outside yourself, you have only one possibility to solve your problems. You must convince others to behave as you see fit. This is common all over the world. You see, blame is notorious for prolonging misery. Without it, one must constantly invent a new problem."

Mary understood the matter only slightly and tried once again to see if Susanne, using the example of her own life, could explain how she manages to be so unhappy.

Susanne believes that, above all else, societal pressure is the culprit. For example, it forces her to work for a living.

Mary latches onto this and asks: "If I understood you correctly, you must work if you wish to have things. Can you explain where the coercion lies?"

"I don't understand your question. That is, nevertheless, the coercion—the fact that I must work."

"If you didn't desire anything, then, this coercion would not exist. Do I understand this correctly?"

"That is nonsense. Without money, one cannot live in Germany. I therefore must earn money."

However, Mary doesn't understand what money is and so must try again to grasp Susanne's problem: "You, therefore, are unhappy because you want to live in Germany?"

"How did you arrive at that?" asks Susanne.

"You are unhappy because you feel pressure from this society to earn money. However, you only need money because you want to live here. I don't understand why you want to live at all in a society that is responsible for your unhappiness. This makes no sense."

Susanne is dumbfounded, and Mary is at a loss.

Mary's way is "hard and paved with stones." The spirit, Ella, tries to teach her various methods for creating a problem. For example, it is useful to set a goal for oneself that one cannot attain. The useless quest would make the destination deliciously unhappy.

With renewed hope, Mary asks: "Ah, if I thus want to experience a problem, which goal should I choose for myself?"

"How about the goal to be free?"

Now, Mary doesn't understand this at all. Since she believes that nobody can take her freedom, she can see no point to this. How can she aspire to gain something she cannot lose?

The spirit guide attempts to give her an example by allowing her—based on her strange behavior—to be placed in an insane asylum. Unfortunately, Mary finds it very nice and even amusing to be there, even if she is unable to distinguish the healthy from the sick. She is only able to determine that sometimes those in white hold back strangely.

At last, Ella, the spirit guide, must release Mary from the asylum, since Mary's inner freedom will no longer accommodate such a confined situation. So, she is involuntarily placed before the door. She regrets it very much, since she was always served such wonderful meals there. How one procures a meal is equal to the pursuit of things that are still unclear.

Through a vision, the spirit guide offers Mary a more direct explanation: "What you have not noticed is that you are already experiencing a problem. You have not noticed it consciously; therefore, it cannot not take hold. Your problem is that you cannot figure out how one feels problems. That you are feeling this as a problem is evidenced by the fact that the many interesting but small things surrounding you in the here and now, you no longer fully notice or enjoy. You cannot wrap your mind around these things, since you are so consumed with your single-minded desire: learning how one feels problems. That has become your problem, and, thus, your perception of the beauties of life has already been altered. This is exactly how problems work. Congratulations, you are one step closer!"

Mary is encouraged by this "great success" to continue. So, Ella, the spirit guide, gives her a new Earth life once again. This time, however, Ella takes away Mary's awareness of her true self—namely, a free, immortal being.

"You are rooted deeply in this life, fully aware of the urge to find happiness and love. Yet, you are firmly convinced that you will only be able to find this contentment outside yourself. That will be the goal, from which all problems will arise. And you will have the feeling of being separate from the rest of creation, of being alone. That will be your biggest problem.

The Earth life, admittedly, also offers the unique possibility to find joy in the small things. Now, for a being with your abilities, this would not even be worth mentioning, but through the aforementioned fundamental problem of your life, you will learn to overlook them."

This life is also the one in which she meets the constantly unhappy Michael. Together, they discover why Michael is often so unhappy. And so, they solve this problem by recognizing that Michael is unhappy only in order to make himself happier. He believes that he must devote his complete attention to the problem at hand, so as not to overlook anything. He wants to perceive the problems, so that he can eliminate them. He believes that only then can he be happy.

However, as time passes, he realizes that the situations in his life are never objectively *good* or *bad*. Whether he sees beauty or ugliness is up to him. He discovers, little by little, that it is he, himself, who decides—based on how he directs his perceptions—how he will feel.

A discussion between a new friend and Michael, who by that time has already put the "trick" to the test, illustrates *the problem*. I took the liberty of modifying the conversation, combining different parts of the book for the sake of simplicity.

The new friend: "I am tired of being constantly criticized. Also, I am sick of people always trying to manipulate me."

Michael: "If, right now, you could stop being criticized and manipulated, what would that do for you?"

"I could be as I am. I could do what I believe is right."

"Why do you want that, to be as you are? What would that do for you?"

"Then, I would be free."

"Why do you want to be free?"

"So that I can do what I want."

"Why do you want to be able to do what you want?"

"Here, we come full circle: because I want to be free."

"Freedom, in itself, has no meaning if nothing new springs from it. As such, freedom cannot be a goal. It is, at most, a prerequisite for attaining something higher."

"The goal then is to be able to do what I want."

"And why do you want to do this?"

"I don't understand the question."

"I think, if you want to do something, then, there must be a reason for it. If you have no motive to do something, then you do nothing."

"The bottom line is: I want to have a really great time! I want to do things that I find joyful and meaningful."

"Your actual goal, then, is to find joy and meaning in everything you do?"

"Just the opposite: I want to devote my time to those things that bring joy and meaning to my life."

"What's the difference?"

"Well, not everything that I do is joyful or meaningful. I have no desire to find everything wonderful, just those things that truly are."

"How can you distinguish the one from the other?"

"I feel it."

"How do you feel it?"

"I just have a knowing if something is meaningful or would bring me joy. It is a certain feeling."

"Suppose you happen to have this feeling surrounding a matter that is actually neither joyful nor meaningful. How then could you distinguish what is really wonderful from what is not?"

"I could not distinguish it."

"Suppose that you have this feeling now. Would there be a further impediment to your happiness?"

"That is difficult; I cannot simply create this feeling right now."

"Okay, then recall a situation when you did have that feeling! Picture in your mind everything just as it was, so you will be able to relive one of the most joyful, most meaningful events in your life. See the world though those eyes—exactly the way you did at that time. And while you see this, pay attention to what you remember. Enjoy this situation fully, tuning into what you are feeling while you see and hear everything just as it was. Do you sense this feeling now?"

"Ah yes, it was really great at that time."

"Now, please, consider once again. If you have this feeling with something that you do, are you still lacking anything?"

"If I have this feeling, I cannot be lacking anything. It is wonderful."

"Is it exactly what you do that is most important, or that you experience this feeling while doing it?"

"You are right. It actually doesn't matter to me what I do specifically. The most important thing is that I have this beautiful feeling. This feeling is my real goal. It makes life worthwhile."

"Until now, you believed that this feeling was conditional on your finding an ideal situation."

"I still think that. I was only able to experience this feeling now because I recalled a joyful event."

"Let's examine this more carefully. You say that you felt it because you recalled it. What exactly happens when recalling? From what does the beautiful feeling originate?"

"I think, by means of the recollection, I direct my attention toward the beautiful feeling."

"Isn't it obvious that this is the only way to have a feeling?"

"What do you mean, the only way?"

"You always experience the feeling, to which your perception aligns itself. Consciously or subconsciously."

"That is logical. Is it so important to recognize this? You act as though it has some crucial meaning."

"That is so. Consider once! If you always experience the feeling, around which your perception centers itself, why not always direct your perception toward this feeling, which you just acknowledged as the true goal—that which makes life worth living?

"Up to now, you have directed your perception toward the ugly because you wanted to get it out the way, in order to then be able to focus on the beautiful. However, you could just as easily perceive the beautiful right now."

"But isn't that simply spiritual denial? Possibly then, I no longer care about the problems that are actually there."

"You will be amazed; actually, the opposite happens. You become increasingly aware of how responsible you are for all your problems. When you recognize your responsibility— and therefore your power—you will find many easy solutions. You will realize that your perspective, in and of itself, reduces the majority of problems and creates more beauty—not only for yourself but for others.

"As long as you direct your perception toward beauty, you are also a thousand times more creative, for you will become receptive. Refusal suppresses creativity. Solutions cannot occur to you when you are in a negative frame of mind. You only feel bad and afraid. If you muster your courage and concentrate on the beautiful, solutions will jump out seemingly from nowhere. If you really want to change the world, then direct your perception toward the beautiful. Through this, your creativity is stimulated, as well as your desire to experience even more beauty.

"You will be able to eliminate problems with greater ease, and you will experience joy in doing this. In this way, so-called reality becomes fun! Also, the more you direct your perception toward the beautiful, the more you become a magnet for good ideas and new solutions. It becomes easy for you to take advantage of all the possibilities that present themselves to you when you recognize that it is your choice whether to perceive your present situation as beautiful or not.

"Simply consider our conversation once again, and decide how you would prefer to direct your perception. Remember what you truly would like: namely, simply that beautiful feeling. You can achieve this from the inside out. It doesn't depend on any external situation. It is your decision, alone, where you direct your perception.

"Most people know this type of positive perception alignment as a vacation. Normally, they are focused on all the things that aren't working right in an attempt to fix them. They direct their attention on what they lack.

"While on vacation, however, everything changes. Wherever they go, they immediately search for beauty. Why not apply this mindset to everyday life?

"If you do, you will attract very different situations in your life. And if you should encounter a so-called problem along the way, you will solve it simply, feeling satisfied that you did something beautiful, not feeling exhausted and drained. Certainly, it is worthwhile to give this a try."

A few words of wisdom from Ella, the spirit guide: "One does not need to summon the love; it is simply there, to be perceived. This can only occur, however, when your perception is aligned with this feeling. Through your anxiety, you direct your perception on everything that can go wrong. Your feelings are based on where you focus your perception. For example, you are never happy because you solved a problem but because, at that moment, your perception is directed toward the sense of well-being. This you can always do."

If you have found inspiration in this snapshot of the adventures of Mary and Michael and would like to further explore this quest toward fulfillment through sheer lust for life, I highly recommend the book, *Mary*, by Ella Kensington. (Please see recommended resources.)

# A Day in the Life
## of a Cosmic Orderer

Someone recently asked me for a list of sample orders, running the gamut from major concerns to the most basic trifle. Such a list I would probably have already compiled—if it were possible. I cannot wrap my mind around it; there are just too many. The request, however, triggered another thought: why is today the way it is? I can, at least, wrap my mind around today!

It is interesting, for example, that I have not received any assignments for graphic design work within the past week, while, at the same time, my publisher has inquired if I would like to write another book—now that I have the time. In addition, a few weeks before, my old ordering buddy, Carsten, criticized my apartment, saying that, even though it was marvelously inexpensive, it was just too small—especially the shower. "Isn't it about time you moved into a larger, but nonetheless cheaper, apartment?" he asked.

Well, on the very day that I finished my latest design assignment, I was offered such an apartment. Now, I can use the free time wonderfully, to prepare the move and to choose some new furniture. I don't have any worries about future assignments either. I know that as soon as I have bought the last lamp, dealt with the last handyman, and am finally settled, the work will come because I will have room for it. I had not ordered this agreeable divine providence, which granted me the time to move and to plan my next book. I didn't even know I needed it. The universe was faster than I. It planned the whole thing for me, in advance.

And so goes this evening. I'm on my way to an office supply store where I want to quickly buy a fax machine that I already saw in another store a few days ago. After that, I want to drive to an evening meditation. I lost my appointment book last week, but I know that, starting tomorrow, my schedule will, once again, be crammed with meetings.

I had already asked my inner voice to remind me of the appointments I needed to meet; however, I also wanted to know whether my calendar would reappear or whether I should call all my business associates to confirm the exact day and time of our meetings. My internal voice announced, "Remain calm; you will find your appointment book by Tuesday."

Nice to know, but I am only human and although the inner voice has never told me nonsense up to now, perhaps she is not infallible and can be mistaken.

Whenever I misplace something, I tune into my inner voice: "Universe, please help me create a mental picture of where I left this item." Sooner than later, the item reappears "all by itself." I am able to retrace my steps so effectively that I literally stumble over the missing object. However, this time, the calendar stayed missing for days. I even called the friend I had visited the last day I remember seeing my calendar. She combed every room in her house but found nothing. I was beginning to fear that my inner voice might be mistaken. Perhaps, my appointment book had somehow ended up in the garbage!

My inner voice said reassuringly, "Remain calm; you will still find your appointment book." Nevertheless, this morning, I awakened in a panic and called everyone with whom I had made appointments to inquire exactly when we had scheduled to meet. My appointments for tomorrow still remained unclear, for I was unable to reach all the relevant parties.

To add further spice, today is my mother's birthday. However, she and a friend are on their way to Italy, and her friend had told me that attempts at a congratulatory call would be pointless because, upon arrival, they would be in the vacation home of their host family for only a few moments, leaving directly for dinner. Also, with such a lengthy car trip, it would be impossible to predetermine what time they would arrive.

"A few moments," I have found, is usually sufficient, and so I programmed my subconscious two days ago to call my mother precisely during those "few moments."

All of these factors are in play this evening as I drive to the office supply store, wanting only to purchase a fax machine and then head over to the meditation group. I have this sense of urgency about buying the fax machine before the meditation starts. But then, it occurs to me that stress and hurry never save time; in fact, they usually cost both time and money. While considering whether or not I will actually save time buying the fax machine today, a back up occurs on the highway. I am relieved of the decision. I hate back ups, so I immediately take an alternate route. Unfortunately, this road is closed due to an overturned truck. The detour leads me to another back up, and so on. I drive so many detours that I suddenly find myself a few blocks from my home! "What was this about?" I ask myself. "Mere chance? Poor sense of direction?" Suddenly, I recall my mother's birthday. "But of course! This odyssey with the car was the universe's way of informing me that now is the perfect time to call my mother in Italy!" I go home, where the telephone number lies.

While looking for a parking space, another idea pops into my head: "Check your answering machine. You will find something far more important than the meditation!" Now, my brain becomes muddled, trying to get a sense of whether this is "genuine advice" from a higher consciousness or whether I am merely indulging an illusion. Through the years, I have learned that over-imaginative ideas feel differently than meaningful hints from the higher consciousness. However, to make this distinction requires much internal vigilance and honest self-assessment. There are times when I excitedly jump to the conclusion: "Wow, this is one of those rare, crystal clear pronouncements from the universe!" However, delighting in such vanity is a sure way to cloud one's judgment, making one vulnerable to chasing after fantasies. I therefore endeavor to allow these sudden intuitions to evolve into something meaningful or senseless, giving me time to figure out leisurely—and preferably without much effort—what is at the heart of the matter.

If following the advice could potentially place me in a risky situation, I always ask for a clear physical sign before I proceed. For example, my internal voice once announced that I should fly to California the following week. I then called the travel agency for the sole purpose of proving to myself that there were no flights available. There was, however, one flight with seats still remaining. Interestingly, it both arrived and returned at optimal times. Still, I continued to fuss about money and the need to substitute this trip for the vacation I had already planned. Well, the bottom line is that these two issues resolved themselves—with no effort on my part—two days later. Therefore, I decided to make the trip and by doing so, met some fascinating people that changed my life.

However, let's return to my current intuition that a message on my answering machine would prevent my attending the meditation. Upon arriving home, the first thing I do is call my mother in Italy. She answers the phone! She tells me that they were held up in a traffic jam and had just arrived. ("Bravo, inner voice! Once again, your timing is perfect!")

In the course of conversation, my mother tells me that she has recently bought a new fax machine and asks if I would like to have her old one. It is a standard paper fax, which is exactly what I need. How fortunate that I did not buy that fax machine a mere ten minutes ago!

Now, for the answering machine . . . I hear my friend's voice, announcing that she has found my appointment book! It had slipped between the cushions of her couch.

I skip the meditation and rush over to my friend's house to retrieve my calendar, since I have so many important appointments starting tomorrow, and I feel that my memory has been less than reliable.

I could have spared myself all the anxiety of this morning had I simply trusted my inner voice.

# *Prerequisites for Successful Ordering*

Are there conditions that must be fulfilled in order to become a recipient of such "divine providence?" Yes and no. You learn the prerequisites simply through experience. The parking space in the center of town appears when needed. Awareness of the right time to make a phone call presents itself, yet awareness of where to find the optimal desk remains elusive. At this point, you will most likely try to figure out how the parking space and the telephone call differed from the desk. On the surface, there is no difference. The only difference is the way you feel. Perhaps you consider the parking space of minor importance and have invested little in the matter surrounding the phone call. However, the pursuit of the perfect desk becomes paramount—this must happen *now*. And thus, the search seems to last forever. In this way, the Cosmic Ordering Service is merciless. As soon as you exhibit the slightest personal strain, you are on your own. Visits to five furniture stores turn up nothing.

Of course, you could no doubt find the optimal desk in nearly any store, but your anxiety blocks creative intuition.

Remember that the universe often works in ways that seem irrational to us. For example, a friend may suddenly call and invite you to lunch at an out-of-the-way place. If you are relaxed and open to impromptu suggestions, you accept. On the way there, you pass an unusual building that attracts your attention. It is a furniture store! Perhaps, you are even a half hour ahead of schedule, which gives you just enough time to saunter inside and practically trip over the perfect desk at just the right price. Now, consider: suppose you had been too stressed to meet your friend for lunch, choosing, instead, to fruitlessly peruse a few more boring furniture shops.

You may ask: how can one tell whether going to lunch would be answering a call from the universe or just giving in to a distraction? Well, you should always presume that hurry and worry are never a productive choice.

Next, you need to tune in to your sense of well-being. Perhaps the very thought of going to lunch makes you feel refreshed in both body and mind, or perhaps you recall that you have an unresolved issue with this friend that you need to discuss. Maybe you have even been carrying an item in your car for the past few months, such as a book or a bottle of wine, that you would like this person to have. These are just some of the subtle ways the universe tries to move you in the right direction.

On the other hand, if the prospect of the meeting makes you feel uneasy, or if you have that sense of "needing" to go for the sake of politeness, you are probably better off persisting in your little quest. Perhaps you find yourself mumbling: "I just want to go somewhere close by and quickly eat in peace, so I have time to visit a few more furniture stores this afternoon."

In summation: go where your energy lies. Just be careful that you do not confuse energy with anxiety. When you are anxious, you cannot hear the universe speak. Thus, your orders cannot be delivered. Stubbornly fixating on your own thought processes, on your own ideas of the way things "should" be, only blocks communication. When you are relaxed and patient, your requests are answered freely because your intuition is attuned to the higher consciousness. You believe that your orders will be addressed all in good time, and so it is.

Although most of the letters that I receive from readers of my first book, *The Cosmic Ordering Service,* enthusiastically report success, from time to time, I do receive letters of disappointment. They usually read something like this: "Since I so urgently need ____, why is the universe not responding? I think this is so unfair! The universe should give me what I need, as I am so poor . . ."

Now, I did not invent this law; I am only the messenger. Once again: those who feel an urgent need for something or wait desperately for it, do not receive it. However, those with a light and airy mind, completely satisfied with what they already have, will receive anything they order. This is not evidence of "life is unfair," but, rather, of the law of attraction. Thoughts of abundance and joy produce abundance and joy, while thoughts of lack and want produce lack and want.

This makes it difficult if you have become entrenched in needy thoughts. The best way to tackle this situation is to actively seek small glimmers of fortune and latch onto them, allowing your sense of abundance to slowly increase. Or you could place an inconsequential order, in which you are not emotionally invested. For example, if you suffer predominantly from a lack of money, try ordering a meeting with a new business contact. If such an order works out, you can feel your way to the next step, ordering some small improvement in your situation. Each small success triggers new opportunities and intuitions, so you make slow but steady progress.

In other words, if you are feeling down on your luck, it makes no sense to request that you become one of the luckiest people alive. This would only work if you feel absolutely no doubt—on any level—that you *can* be one of the luckiest people alive and have sufficient trust to simply place the order and forget about it. Such a gigantic shift in mindset goes against human nature; so, again, I suggest that you content yourself with baby steps. In this way, you will learn to trust your intuition.

Today, I received a call from a television producer, proposing the following concept: random folks would pass their orders onto me, and I would give them up to the universe (since I am the "professional orderer"). Two days later, on the next show, the recipients would report what had transpired. I was quite baffled by his suggestion, wondering how the subjects were supposed to receive intuitions "on demand," placing them at the right place at the right time. They would probably experience the most stressful two days of their lives, pausing at each street corner with the thought: "Was that a hint that I should turn left instead of right? That arrow blinks so beautifully it pulls me onward. Yet, from the right, a strange wind blows. Perhaps I should go that way." And as for me, I could imagine nothing worse than to be under the pressure to place orders for others, while the public looked on anxiously. I could never release the orders with the necessary tranquility.

I suppose it would be different if I truly were a "professional orderer," and were therefore independent of the expectations of others. If I could then matter-of-factly order: "Well, Universe, there, you have invented something fine, indeed. Now, take heed as to its outcome. Manifest for him/her the entire order at once. I look forward to the certainty of great results." But unfortunately, I do not have the nerve.

Allegedly, a person with mental control has power over mentally disorganized humans. If I could stand thusly before the universe with the clear conviction that the orders must function, this would, no doubt, have more weight than the fear, doubt, and stress of those guinea pigs from the audience. Since, however, I do not have such a conviction, I suggested to the producer that they should still present several orders, with the idea that they would soon learn that stress and pressure are not conducive to successful ordering.

A by-product of cosmic ordering is that you learn to be blatantly honest—even with yourself. If you imagine that something exists where nothing, in fact, exists, you will remain on the wrong track, never arriving at the right place at the right time. This becomes readily apparent when you compare successful with unsuccessful orders, asking yourself: "What was different with me and within my thoughts?"

In order to become a consistently successful orderer, you must recognize your true motivations again and again and trade long-held beliefs for new and improved ideas. It is also necessary to learn to distinguish that genuine sense of well-being (which originates from the soul) from a superficial feeling of contentment (which originates from the ego). Finally, you must be prepared to take action.

Once, I was lined up in a traffic back up, waiting to enter the freeway. The street was packed with newly fallen snow, and nothing was moving. It wasn't clear exactly why nothing was moving; the only thing that was clear was that everyone in that traffic jam wanted to get on the freeway. I placed an order that the jam would dissolve as quickly as possible; however, I immediately had a bad feeling. Still, nothing moved. Many of the drivers had even turned off their motors. I had this growing feeling that I should just drive past all of this—but how? Suddenly, my inner voice announced, "Drive along the shoulder!" Well, I drove, amazed that the other drivers allowed me to pass without contention. Soon, the ramp onto the freeway came into view. Three cars were stranded on the incline, which led to the freeway. They were stuck in the snowy slush. All the other drivers were lined up dutifully behind them, doing nothing. In view of this situation, it was not at all embarrassing for me to drive in front of the waiting cars and organize a bumper-to-bumper line of cars which then pushed and dislodged the first, then the second, and finally the third stuck vehicle. Then I was pushed up the ramp and so on. Eventually, the slippery mush was completely dispersed, and cars could travel freely once again.

Such situations have taught me that it is not enough to merely catch the ball; I must be willing to run with it. I cannot tell you how many times I have ordered something only to let a suitable opportunity slip through my fingers.

## *Everything Good Comes from Within*

The more positive experiences I have with cosmic ordering—the more large and small "miracles" I have under my belt—the better my life becomes. To be perfectly honest, I still occasionally doubt what I experience (not too intelligent of me, I might add!). Nevertheless, I am at a point where I can look back on a repertoire of small positive experiences that have transpired within the last few days realizing: "If *that* worked out the day before yesterday, then surely *this* is possible today!"

By nature, it is difficult for me to hold onto "physical miracles," if you will, particularly if the manifestations occurred several months ago or longer. Intellectually, my memory remains intact, but physically—and psychically— the awareness becomes cloudy over time. On this level, the experiences often become unreal to me, allowing some of the old doubts to reemerge. On the other hand, the many ordinary mini-miracles that have colored my most recent days are still alive in feeling. It is exactly these that help me, in such moments of doubt, to recall that so much more is possible. This realization provides fertile ground for the next small miracle to blossom. This lends credence to all those who repeat: "Be grateful for what you have." If you fail to acknowledge the miraculous in the everyday, you deplete the cosmic energy and thus, have nowhere to begin. It is like trying to fly a plane with no fuel. The more confident you become in the Cosmic Ordering Service, the less likely anything will go wrong.

Here's an example of an ordinary mini-miracle: an extremely bad case of cramps—the likes of which I had not experienced in over ten years—seized me at a most unfavorable time. Of course, I immediately urged my body to become well: "Now, we have not succumbed to this in over ten years. This malady is a thing of the past. Stop this immediately! You are mistaken; it cannot be! We do not have cramps." Nonetheless, the best that I received through these efforts was a thirty-second respite. No sooner had I convinced myself that the cramps were gone then they would return. And so, I vacillated for a while between pain and respite.

I have heard it said that if you give yourself permission to focus your complete attention for five minutes on a negative experience, you can transcend it. However, this has rarely worked for me, and at that moment, I had the impression that the pain would only become worse if I allowed my thoughts to embrace it. So, taking the opposite tack, I went back to work. The pain persisted. As I considered poisoning myself with pharmaceutical products (in other words: to take a painkiller), I made one final attempt to communicate with the inner voice: "You have already solved so many of my problems. What can we do about this?" Then, I forced myself to concentrate on my work for five minutes.

Suddenly, the memory of a conversation about the positive effects of drinking alcohol presented itself to me. This discussion had transpired two years ago, and by that time, I had already given up drinking for many years. The other person's argument had been that some people are so externally and internally stressed that the relaxation benefit of an occasional drink far outweighs its damaging effects. In such cases, the body is so grateful for this relaxation that it compensates by restricting the damage done to it. (The dosage for this beneficial effect does vary greatly from person to person!) The argument was meant as a counter to alcohol-bashers, suggesting that they become more tolerant of a person's choice to drink.

"Okay," I said to myself. "Let's put this argument to the test right now." The alcohol would certainly have to do some serious relaxation in my case! The only disadvantage, which is also the main reason why I no longer drink, is that alcohol makes me extremely sleepy and dizzy. I was afraid of this consequence, since I still had so much work to do. Nonetheless, the pain was far worse than any possible grogginess, and I was finding it difficult to work through the pain anyway. Bring on the beer!

The first gulp went right to my head, and I waited for the fatigue to overtake me. After a few more sips, my pain was nearly gone. Now, the absence of pain produced so much joy and enthusiasm that all those feel-good hormones must have countered the effect alcohol normally has on me. I drank two whole beers (for a non-drinker, this is a lot of alcohol in a short time) and nevertheless felt better and better. I was fully alert and able to concentrate. I could not perceive the smallest reduction in my energy or cognition; in fact, if anything, they increased. My work went well.

Admittedly, this was an extremely simple approach, and for someone else, it may not have worked. However, the art lies in the ability to receive the correct idea at the correct time. For me, this experience provided confirmation that intuition (or the universe) offers advice in ways that are often overlooked, so I need to remain completely open.

More recently, not so simple a case occurred. I had been in a tired mood for two days, ever since I had discovered that all three curves of my biorhythms were at the low point. At first, I looked at this as a self-fulfilling prophecy. Simply by chance, however, I found out that a good friend of mine, whose biorhythms always run exactly contrary to mine, was at a high point. "Well," I figured, "nothing mysterious here. Perhaps the curves are accurate."

That morning, the listlessness was overwhelming, and nothing but confusion filled my brain. I decided that this was certainly not an acceptable condition in which to begin the day, and so, I immediately turned to my favorite self-motivation program. Although this rarely fails to work, this time, it only made me feel even more confused. I sat quietly and observed what was happening in my mind. I believed that this was the quintessential low point of my cycle, and that I needed to uncover the reason behind it in order to change direction. However, I was unable to do so. In fact, all the self-analysis only triggered further dark thoughts. I recalled the ghastliest theories of the esoteric scene:

"If the Earth's magnetic field were directed to zero, then all of humanity would become insane because human emotions are dependent upon the magnetic field of the Earth."

(Aha! It was probably moving in that direction, and my brain was already producing disorders.)

"At the present time, chaotic energies prevail upon the Earth, and more and more people are becoming addicted to the inner chaos." (Well, there we have it! I had laughed at the allegedly chaotic energies—from which I had never noticed anything—for too long. Now, they had caught up with me after all!)

"The antenna field, HAARP, in Alaska emits dissonant energies that influence the consciousness of all people." (If that be the case, why should I be immune?)

That third dark theory really struck me. I began to analyze where the crisis would come from, and this generated even darker thoughts. Whatever one directs her energy upon becomes strong. I had found a plausible reason for the bad feelings as well. Well, bravo! I had convinced myself through the use of some time-worn theories that I could not improve. Such rubbish! I had fed myself with alleged "reasons" for my condition and had called it analyzing. I had to take the opposite approach right away, so I channeled my energy into creating positive thoughts. Yet, the repetition of positive mantras produces nothing at all if one does not fully believe. I had already convinced myself of every possible negative. Finally, I spoke, once again, with the universe: "You who gave me that wonderful tip concerning the use of alcohol for my pain and eliminated all side effects can certainly succeed in restoring order to my thoughts and feelings. I would like to be able to think clearly, powerfully, freely, and happily. Tell me what I must do in order to achieve this immediately!" I expected, in response, a complicated set of instructions or a clever trick, such as the suggestion of a useful book to read or to meditate a certain way, with particular music. However, the answer is always presented differently than one expects. As soon as I decided to hold fast to my desire to restore my thought processes to lucidity, power, freedom, and joy, I leaned upon infinite possibilities and abilities. At that moment, something "clicked" inside of me, and everything became clear. The chaos disappeared. I was completely bewildered.

Unlike the pain, which I had anticipated with fear, the chaotic thoughts did not return. My "counter" had been reset, "clicked" into place. I knew within two minutes that I would require nothing further, and that the chaos would not return (at least, not in the near future). With this internal click, a creative intoxication had been stimulated. For the remainder of the day, I felt extraordinarily lucid, positive, and powerful. I sketched so furiously for an hour straight that I covered pages with new ideas, even pulling pieces of scrap paper from my pocket to keep up with my creativity.

Lest you, the reader, perceive this as just a momentary flash, allow me to share with you that everything is still wonderful with me. Today was super, crammed with creativity. Now, it is late at night, and I still have the desire to write. Life can be wonderful!

I do hope that this example does not cause you to cry: "Nothing has 'clicked' for me! What am I doing wrong?"

I have practiced developing my "clicks" for ten years, and my experiences should by no means become your yardstick. The only path to finding your own way is through communication with your inner voice.

Our most important commonality, as human beings, is that we find the best solutions for all our problems in our own interior. In the outside world, we can receive advice and inspiration from other people, but even then, we mirror ourselves in the mutual exchanges we attract. The final authority is always the self.

Let's presume, dear reader, that you find yourself in internal chaos and have not, as of yet, perceived even the slightest communication from your inner voice. Nonetheless, you build on the simple fact that s/he at least hears you and understands your intention. A suitable response could then come within the next few days in the form of a chance meeting or an appropriate comment. Or, perhaps, you open—purely by chance—a book at exactly the right passage, which helps you at the moment. Or, or, or . . .

Maybe your inner voice prescribes peppermint tea with raspberry ice and ketchup as a remedy for your internal chaos. So what? That is super advice! I would accept this immediately, since nothing terrible could come from it.

On the other hand, if the inner voice should somehow announce: "Travel to Alaska and freeze the chaos; then, you can return," I would caution you to demand substantial proof of the effectiveness of this "cure." Otherwise, I would suggest that you buy yourself a postcard of Alaska and meditate over it, for intuitions can also be total nonsense. To put the intuition concerning the peppermint tea, raspberry ice, and ketchup to the test poses little risk; however, to travel to Alaska is quite another matter. In that case, you need to be sure.

Even an expert remote viewer like Joseph McMoneagle, the number one remote viewer of the Pentagon, said that he is only 65 percent accurate in the use of remote viewing. In 35 percent of all cases, imagination and nonsense cloud the outcome. (Sixty-five percent is still huge.) Suppose a general was abducted into another country, and you needed to find his exact location by means of remote viewing. What percentage of the time would you be successful? One to 0 percent. McMoneagle is 65 percent accurate! Of interest is his book, *Mind Trek*. (Please see recommended resources.)

Even McMoneagle cannot always distinguish intuition from imagination. He can only be sure when what was viewed psychically is actually witnessed at the physical location.

I once conducted an interview with McMoneagle, from which I learned that a remote viewer, honored with the highest military awards and with twenty-one years professional experience working for all of the United States Secret Service agencies, doesn't necessarily do better than I. I, too, cannot always distinguish intuition from imagination. Admittedly, there is usually a difference in feeling between the two but not always. Sometimes, my inner voice speaks so clearly that I can't help but recognize it. Other times, I can only guess if what I "heard" was real. With peppermint tea and raspberry ice, I am ready for the experiment (even with the ketchup). However, with Alaska, I want extra vacation money (through winnings, investments, or a sudden surge in contracts), the ideal travel agency, etc. In other words, I need a serious showing of signs and coincidences to convince me to do more than just buy that postcard.

Yet, you must decide what will make you happy. You needn't listen to me. Travel calmly to Alaska and send me a postcard when you arrive. Most importantly: will it help? The measure of the effectiveness is the measure of the truth! If, in Alaska, you come into particularly good contact with your inner voice, then the journey is worthwhile.

But consider: You can travel half way around the world in body, but if you are not properly aligned in spirit, you will not recover anywhere!

# *Will I Become Too Good If I Listen to the "Divine" within Me?*

If you have not asked yourself this question, I congratulate you. I held onto this fear for many years, and only recently was I able to release it. If I recall anything from all the spiritual seminars and lectures I have attended it is this: my ego must be destroyed. Evil people will rob my life of joy, but I should remain good. It is always the ego that triggers the baser desires. I should not desire to remain an individual "water drop," but should strive to become "one with the sea." In other words, I should give up my individuality freely. And is this supposed to be fun? Definitely not. It is only extremely "good." The "good" water drops return to the sea, while the "evil" ones splash around on their own without asking the sea's permission. This reminds me of the saying: "Good girls go to heaven; bad girls go everywhere."

Well, I get around quite a bit, and I'd like it to remain so. Farewell, sea; I would rather remain a drop!

In the spiritual scene, I actually jumped around a lot to escape sensationalism. Whoever cares to penetrate through even the most transparent surface quickly goes beyond all castles in the air and such things that act as surrogate miracles for so many. Ironically, in this way, I found answers that nobody had been able to give me. In the final analysis, I learned to search for the answers within myself. It was around this time that I also stopped being afraid of becoming too "good."

One evening, I attended a seminar where the speaker professed herself to be "an ambassador of the risen masters." Saint Germain (supposedly one of the masters being channeled through the speaker) addressed the audience, and Lady So-and-So (unfortunately the name escapes me—not being a known master to me) also greeted the crowd. Many people lined up to ask these risen masters what—in light of all the problems here on Earth—does God actually do in heaven? Does he do anything to try to alleviate all this sorrow?

Replied Lady So-and-So: "Consider that, perhaps, the blame does not rest with God but with us. God has given us the power to thwart these problems; however, instead of using our free will to develop this power, we use it to sit passively by.

"Developing our power does not mean that we must become world leaders. We must simply begin to build paradise from the building blocks of our own lives. These personal steps lay the most effective path to universal paradise." So much for Lady So-and-So: her presence evaporated as quickly as it had sprung forth. I found her words extraordinary, however. They reminded me of that well-known medium who, for years, channeled the archangel Gabriel (or was it Michael?). In this case, as well, the utterances themselves were noble and helped a great many people.

At that time, the aforementioned reverse speech therapy had already appeared on the scene (see chapter 6). So, the medium visited David Oates (the discoverer of this phenomenon), in the hopes that he could provide evidence that she really was channeling the archangel.

In reverse speech, the client can be instructed by the therapist on the appropriate places to listen. All one needs to know is when to listen, for which tone, and with which word the key sentence begins in order to ascertain—even with untrained ear—what was "actually" said. Well, in this case, the medium, by listening to her own speech played backwards, was able to determine that it was not the archangel speaking at all, but her own inner voice.

Now, you might think that she would be proud to discover that the wisdom that had provided so many with such discerning insights was truly *hers*. But no, she was dreadfully annoyed and embarrassed that it had not been the archangel speaking through her.

Not that I could care less if it had been the archangel, the higher self, or Kermit the Frog. The intuitions, themselves, were what mattered. If they were good and useful for someone, who cares from whence they came?

This is why I simply say that I order from the universe. I have no idea with whom I am truly communicating. It could be the archangel Gabriel who executes the orders, or, or . . . I only need to know that it works.

Now, I must honestly share with you, Dear Reader, yet another experience. I was taking part in a meditation group where I felt wonderfully relaxed and blissful. For the first time during meditation, I was able to perceive different types of energies. Specifically, I felt the energy of what I perceived to be Saint Germain—the energy was so similar to what had come forth at the seminar.

To better understand this, think of the way you remember very familiar people. Most likely, you create not only a mental picture but also a unique feeling. You are experiencing the physical qualities of the person and his/her aura simultaneously. In the same way, meditative energies can have individual colorings and sensations attached to them.

This is a phenomenon that I am, to this day, rarely able to perceive, yet on this particular evening, it became marvelously clear. Group meditations have the advantage over solo meditation in that the collective energy is innately stronger. For someone of a duller nature like me, the group setting can provide a kind of energy shower to the psyche.

One year later, I experienced such an energy shower at another group meditation, in a different setting with different participants. Suddenly, this strange feeling came over me, allowing me to perceive a special and clearly individual energy, which again reminded me of Saint Germain. While I was marveling over the unlikelihood of so specific an awareness, the group leader announced: "Some of you may already be aware of it; the master Saint Germain has come into our presence." A shiver traveled down my spine.

Admittedly, I have had no more of these visitations since that time. However, I refrain from judging those who claim the ability to channel repeatedly, almost at will, this or that archangel or risen master. Maybe they do it, maybe they don't. The fact that I cannot regularly channel these energies does not mean that others cannot.

On the other hand, what does it matter if they are channeling individual personas or simply tapping into the collective consciousness, the personification of God, the universe, or whatever? If the outcome is positive, creating a sense of well-being and connectedness to the higher energy source, what else matters?

When faced with such discoveries, I simply tune into my inner self. If something feels good and right for me, then, I am content. It does not matter to me from which energy or deity my intuitions spring. In fact, I now understand that if I were to know the exact source of my insights, the whole process would no longer be fun for me. There was a time, however, when I thwarted these unknown energies out of the fear that they would rob me of my ego. Thank God that we human beings are capable of change and that the energies adapt to us.

The universal energy changes as we human beings change. As we become more liberated and fluid, the universal energy does also. Intuitions and so-called transmissions were, at one time, strict and imperious because we were strict and imperious. Now, the energies flow more freely, becoming more pliable from year to year. The information from "the other side" will doubtlessly remain constant. It is the evolving human who will translate it differently.

The more relaxed the human, the more lucid are the transmissions. It is not necessary to relinquish the ego to become receptive. What we can do is set aside that part of the ego that controls us, the part that triggers the knee-jerk reaction to defend ourselves from being re-directed. Were it not for old, safe patterns that compel us to run again and again into the same dead end, we would gladly take a new direction. By releasing these outdated patterns, we become more of who we are, not less. Quite clearly: the less fear we have, the more freely we can decide what we desire. Without fear, we are no longer pushed into actions—or reactions—towards what we don't really want.

By turning into the servant, the newly cleansed ego helps us find more options in life. We can be who we want to be. The old ego maintained control by relieving us of decision making through fear and automatic reactions. What's wrong with relinquishing that?

Since re-defining ego-annihilation (see chapter 3), I am no longer afraid of it. I can still remain an individual "drop," setting aside useless fears and patterns while retaining those aspects of myself that I admire. In this way, I actually become more of myself, not less.

Nonetheless, the question still remains: through this process, can one actually become too good? The spiritual advisors of today dedicate their lives to interpreting and sharing what is communicated to them by the inner voice. Does this wisdom come from an ascended master or from the advisor's own innate divinity? This point has always baffled me. Why should I be led by another's divine guidance when I have my own? I want to decide for myself! Now, this divine part of me probably only has goodness within it, but scarcely do I remember to go inward, listening to the voice that whispers: "Be quiet and good and modest" and so on.

Those who live so always speak of how "giving in" to the divine will has simplified their lives. I have always suspected that this has something to do with being good. Why should I desire to live according to the divine will? I want to live after my own will or not at all! So be it. "Yet, the divine will and yours are nonetheless one," murmured the gurus.

For many years, my ego asserted that the divine will was really modest goodness ("Good girls go to heaven . . ."), while my own will was not so lofty (". . . bad girls go every-where").

Recently, I came to understand what it truly means to be at one with the divine will. It certainly does not mean that I must abandon all fun, bending my will to a narrow-minded God. However, it does mean that God will shape my will to become who I really am as soon as I order from the universe my deepest desire.

The divine will is said to be the fearless part of us. This part has different motives than the ego, which operates mostly out of fear. If I do something from a place of pure joy in living, fearless abandon, and abundance for the sole purpose of creating good in my life or someone else's, then I am operating through divine will.

On the other hand, if I act out of fear of loss or the desire to outdo others, then my ego is propelling me. The fear of becoming "too good" is therefore sheer nonsense because that would mean that I am afraid of acting out of joy in living, confident abandon, and love.

Here's a real-life example: in 1995, I planned to do two things. I wanted to publish a partly spiritual, partly secular magazine, reporting positive news. Although I wanted to do this for my personal enjoyment, I also wanted to earn money. Since everyone predicted that this could never turn out all right, due to the glut of magazines already on the market, I thought that perhaps a kind of "spiritual guidance office" might bridge the market gap. I therefore started the magazine and partnered with a friend to open the agency simultane-ously.

Running a spiritual guidance office was not exactly a dream come true for either one of us. We merely believed that it would fill a niche market, providing us with enough money and space to pursue our real interests. So, we diligently explored the market. Nonetheless, the divine in us seemed to be taking a siesta as far as the agency was concerned. No suitable inspirations of any kind presented themselves. The business did little but cost us considerable money in advertising.

Meanwhile, the magazine just felt right, filling the emptiness inside with true joy and fulfillment. I faced the work with enthusiasm. There, the universe woke up. It poured out miracles on the grandest scale. From the first edition, which I photocopied and distributed single-handedly, sprang the rather successful magazine, *Solar Wind*.

The divine will, therefore, is that I create paradise from my life on Earth. If I strive to do this, I am supported continuously, as evidenced by hundreds—even thousands of "coincidences" that bring forth outcomes far better than I could even imagine. If, however, I decide by virtue of my free will to live my life in mistrust and fear, focusing my energy on safe but dismal occupations that do not inspire me, I am no longer operating on the same frequency as the divine will and cannot be supported.

When I was in high school, I had a dear friend who—unlike me—knew exactly what she wanted to do with her life at the age of sixteen. She knew that she did not want to go to college, and after flunking her final exams, rationalized that she did not need a high school diploma either. She told her parents that she wanted to break away from school and become a secretary. Her parents ran a lucrative business and had hoped that their daughter would "make something of herself." Therefore, her father threatened to disown her if she dropped out of school. Her mother, hoping the family could reach a compromise, suggested: "If that is truly what you want to do, then enroll in a business school where you can learn typing and stenography."

Well, that is precisely what she did. The daughter of wealthy parents became a secretary. When she moved into her first apartment—a tiny efficiency financed by her meager start-up salary, she was as pleased as punch. Admittedly, her parents must have used some of their influence to help her, for she became the executive secretary for a major business owner in record time. Eventually, she became a junior manager in the family business.

That being said, her decision to follow her inner voice gave her the opportunity to gain much more practical business experience than she ever could have in college. She now lives her life fearlessly, with the knowledge that life situations link together to achieve the best possible outcome as long as her will is aligned with that of the divine. This came about simply by her willingness to learn who she really was, independent from the expectations of others. The surprising result of this was that her relationship with her parents— because of her added value as a fully self-aware individual—became even better.

Compare this to the story of a man I know, named Hector. He, too, grew up amidst a wealthy family business; however, Hector never took the time to figure out who he really was. To his way of thinking, such self-searching could only lead to a lower standard of living than he could achieve via the family business. Therefore, he learned only the bare minimum of what he would need to be useful in this capacity and settled into a support position directly under his father. This was precisely what the family had expected, so they viewed Hector as a "good man."

However, since he had never learned to assert himself as a free agent, he had no idea of what it takes to be a leader. Result: a mere two years after his father retired, Hector has nearly run the once successful business into the ground. Now, his fear increases as the realization gradually sinks in that the high times are coming to a close.

Unfortunately, he does not—yet—see this as an opportunity to begin again, to search for his true self, his true joy. He would rather sit in front of the TV with a bottle of beer, mourning the "good old days." The divine will and the will of this man are clearly not in synch. Presently, however, he is afraid—as I used to be—of his inner voice. He is afraid that it will lead him into some exhausting, low-paying undertaking that will force him to lower his standard of living forever. In reality, if a high standard of living is paramount to his sense of well-being, his inner voice will not lead him away from this, but because he knows so little about himself, he fears the worst. He is not willing to take the risk to look inward, seeing it as a journey with no return.

Hector has told me, specifically, that he is afraid to stare down a truth that he has suspected all along: he truly wants to be a sculptor. Yet, sculptors do not make much money, and poverty is Hector's biggest fear. I have suggested that he should still look inward to determine if, perhaps, he could develop a side job or even a rewarding hobby from his true talents. Even this, he does not dare, so afraid is he of his own depths. He does not understand that the sky behind the clouds, burdening the soul, is always blue. I wish he could discover that nothing bad can ever come from bringing the ego with all its fears into more agreement with the so-called divine will—with all its zeal.

Remember: know yourself, and you will be supported! You can start anywhere, at any time, meeting the divine will with as much commitment as you can muster. Many people put it off, due to the mistaken belief that they must go from 0 to 100 percent immediately. Nothing could be further from the truth. If you have 10 percent—or 2 percent—start there.

It is not necessary to live a "good" life, but only the life which you would truly like to live. I am convinced that you could open a brothel and be supported if that were your true desire. In such a case, you would no doubt have the best brothel in the entire city and quickly, too!

To bring this chapter full circle, I will return to this evening's lecture, which greatly inspired me because it offered proof of the material presence of a universal force, manifesting our wishes with ease. From a different perspective, the speaker was actually supporting my belief in the Cosmic Ordering Service! I felt inspired to write this chapter the minute I arrived home, but it was already midnight and I wanted to go to sleep even more. Enter: divine will, which does not, in many cases, correspond to our primal expectations.

Actually, I didn't even "expect" to attend the lecture at all! I had wanted to go elsewhere, but an out-of-town acquaintance called, saying he really wanted to attend this lecture, and asked if he could stay overnight with me. His enthusiasm inspired me to change my plans, and I went along. I am glad I did so, for the event inspired the very words you are reading right now!

Nonetheless, it is late. (I cannot look at the clock, for I know that if I do, I will become instantly tired.) The minute I arrived home, my body was crying out to go to bed, but my inner voice said: "Now, you are in a completely inspired state in which you have everything you need to write. You need only to turn on your computer, and all tiredness will vanish. You can write ten pages effortlessly. If you go to sleep, however, you will have to recall to mind tomorrow what you wanted to write. You will have to force yourself, and the whole process will become arduous. Nonetheless, the choice is yours: sacrifice sleep now and take advantage of the effortless inspiration or face an arduous memory-lashing tomorrow or perhaps risk losing the chapter altogether."

Okay, okay, I made my choice, and I am surprised that the page counter already indicates number 8. Nevertheless, there are times when I ask myself: who actually is in charge here? Is it still me?

This evening, I wanted to be somewhere else. The out-of-town acquaintance ended up staying overnight with another friend. It seemed his sole purpose in coming into town was to lure me to that lecture. Besides, I had wanted to go to bed early. How are my desires being answered here? Still, I have free will. Why did I decide to go this way? Simply put, this choice had more energy attached to it, and it seemed more fun. To insist on proceeding according to my plans would have been far less satisfying.

The vibrant life is always haphazard and spontaneous. The more firm the rule, the less alive is the life. However, when life completely loses its structure, the concept backfires, and everything becomes more arduous instead of easier.

You need to determine the correct measure of all things for yourself, based upon your sense of well-being.

Most importantly, you must find out who you really are and what you truly want. To do this, you need to coordinate the timing of your actions with your intuition and sense of well-being. You must be flexible and open to signs regarding the best times to take action. This is most important. If you attempt to force outcomes at the wrong time, you will waste much energy. You will recognize the "correct time" by the flow of energy: events will transpire seamlessly and without effort.

Those around you may not understand this way of living and may even deem it egotistical. Simply allow them their own opinions, saying to yourself: "It is not my task to recognize the paths of others; it is my task to recognize my own way, which I will follow with joy."

# Conclusive Evidence
## of the Cosmic Force

This evening, I attended a lecture on "light food" by Jasmuheen, the Australian proponent of "breatharianism," or living without food. Since 1993, she has lived without eating and occasionally also without drinking. When most people hear this for the first time, they indignantly proclaim: "Impossible!" When they hear of it a second time, their response is usually more matter-of-fact: "Oh, I heard about that before." If they hear of the phenomenon still again, after some time has passed, they usually say something like: "Oh, yes . . . that has become quite common . . ."

Four hundred years ago, all were indignant when Galileo Galilei declared that the sun did not revolve around the Earth. In more recent times, humanity was certain it would never visit the moon. Today, people in the West find it difficult to believe that a human being could live without food and water.

In India, however, hardly anyone finds such a thing surprising, according to Jasmuheen. There, many yogis can and do "live on light," and hardly anyone considers it miraculous. "He just lives on Prana, which springs from the God force, so what?"

When Jasmuheen began the process of learning to live without material food, she had no intention of receiving such worldwide attention. Her inner voice (or the channeled risen masters: take your pick) told her that the time was ripe for a deep outpouring of spiritual knowledge throughout the media, that a kind of "communal receptivity" was developing. In such a climate, Jasmuheen's experiences would naturally resonate.

Nonetheless, the topic of "light food" constitutes only a small part of her seminars, the heart of which are "inner leadership." Jasmuheen sees herself as an ambassador of inspiration, introducing people to their inner divinity, showing them that anything is possible if they believe in it.

As evidence that the time is ripe to build a bridge between the spiritual and the doubters, scientific studies concerning light food are popping up all over the globe.

In England, another proponent of light food received the intuition to go under clinical observation for six weeks. During that time, he neither ate nor drank. Scientists and doctors oversaw every step of the process, administering myriad tests. (See recommended resources.) Jasmuheen, herself, says it does not matter whether one lives solely on Prana or not. What does matter is the contact one establishes with his/her own inner divinity. The more people discover God within themselves, the sooner we will attain peace on Earth.

Prana, or light food, is an effective way to prove the existence of a cosmic force because if Jasmuheen and others can live for years without food or drink, there must be a powerful energy source sustaining them.

Nonetheless, if a human being attempts to live without food or drink when this does not fit into his/her world view—and presently, this applies to 99 percent of all people—such abstinence will do more harm than good. There are thousands of ways to prove the existence of a cosmic force. One should find the right way for oneself; otherwise, no progress will be made.

For example, if the cosmic force can replace physical food for a particular person, she believes it is so. The only barrier to our possibilities is belief (i.e., belief in the possibilities of our orders to the universe). Jasmuheen also sends orders to the universe but in a different manner. She believes in angels.

The energies which she calls angels don't have free will. They must serve the divine will and, in so doing, also serve us if we are following the divine within. The angels cannot serve us if we are commanded by our egos.

Again, to clarify: the ego is the part of us that desires something in order to appear more important than others, in order to control others, in order to satiate inferiority complexes, to wield power, etc. The ego is motivated by fear and self-doubt. Angels cannot serve these negative emotions. They serve only love. That is, they serve every desire that stems from love, trust, and childlike joy.

A concrete example: a man orders a bigger apartment for himself because his brother has just moved into a bigger apartment, and the man has spent his life trying to prove he can do whatever his brother does. This desire springs from fear, whether acknowledged or not. That is okay, but he will have to obtain the apartment on his own.

Example 2: A man orders a bigger apartment out of love for the neighborhood and the desire to have more fun, being able to invite more friends over, having a larger space to share with them. In this case, the angels must help him because he wishes for something from a place of love, not fear.

In a case like this, the best thing to do is make a list of everything that would bring you joy and task the angels to bring you "this or something better."

Jasmuheen and her partner did exactly that when neither had time to even look for a new apartment. In thought and with the imagination, they summoned the "house-hunting angel" and told her exactly what they wanted, sending her forth with the words: "Go and bring us exactly this or something better!" Then, they did nothing at all except go about their daily business. In short order, a residence was offered to them in an area where it would not have occurred to them to look! It was exactly what they had requested. Even the color of the walls matched their order. Enthusiastically, they thanked the angel.

Everything you order with love and without fear will come to pass. If it does not come, seek the reason from your inner voice. Remember the old saying: "Keep an eye on your thoughts; they could become your destiny." Concentrate on the love and joy of life and invite the divine will—or the angels—to clean up your thoughts. Most likely, you will come across the optimal meditative technique, a new relaxing hobby, or something else that will bring ease and structure to your thoughts.

According to Jasmuheen, it achieves little to think: "I am grateful for the abundance that now enters my life" in an attempt to produce abundance if your energy body is consumed with chaos, sending the opposite message to each and every cell (i.e., poverty, tribulation, limitation). A possible trick of Jasmuheen to balance the energy body is to tap into the sexual energy. Sit down for five minutes daily and send your sexual energy upward, along your spinal column. You can support this physically by tightening the muscles between the anus and genitals. While inhaling, send the energy upward, along the spine. When exhaling, send the energy downward, along the front of your body. While doing this, think: "Sex, spirit, heart in perfect balance."

This practice is quite simple; however, it does rearrange the energy body. As a result, your heart opens, creating a kind of cosmic telephone line to your higher self. (Remember, you are the drop of water that reconnects itself to the ocean, not to lose your individuality but to become more of who you are.)

A concluding tip from Jasmuheen: there are people who are ambassadors of the perfection of heaven. One recognizes them by the fact that they are always healthy, since they comprehend from the inner voice and the divine will that physical ailments are superfluous. These people meditate daily. (For an hour or for two to three sessions of twenty minutes each.) The techniques used are of no importance, for they realize it is up to them to discover what works best for them. They have positive relationships with their family and friends. They have a sense of purpose to life and enjoy it to the fullest.

Finally, remember that you can abandon this reality whenever you choose, simply by the fact that you no longer wish to be here. Only when you are completely happy with everything here do you hold the liberty of choice in your hands. And whoever understands *who* she is, understands that she can do *everything*.

# Meditation for the Lazy

What I am about to propose to you is a long way from "serious" meditation. A better term for it would be "medi-playing." Simply try it once and determine whether it works for you or not.

If you want to allow yourself some fun, you can look over all my "rules" and do the opposite. Maybe you will fare just as well, even better, or worse. Everything is okay. Find out what works for you. The only criterion is that you make progress.

And now, here is the brilliantly simple medi-playing, the all-purpose, effective meditation for the lazy:

*Rule 1:* Sit down comfortably. It does not matter how. The back does not need to be straight. In fact, nothing has to be any particular way, except that it is better to sit than to lie down: one is more apt to lose concentration and fall asleep in a supine position.

*Rule 2*: You can change your position at anytime if it becomes uncomfortable. Also, scratching and fidgeting are permitted.

*Rule 3*: Since our goal is to go inward, stimuli from the outside are counterproductive. Therefore, no music should be played because, then, we listen to the outside instead of our own inner voice. Certainly, no other people, animals, or plants should be in the area, for a part of our attention— even subconsciously—cannot prevent being pulled toward this other life energy. (If the other being is meditating with us, that is all right.)

*Rule 4*: Thoughts do not have to be pushed away.

*Rule 5*: We affirm (reinforce intellectually) only those things in which we are already confident. We do not try to "convince" ourselves of anything. Now, here's the real key of medi-playing for the lazy: we think positively about what we already believe, or even more simply, we focus on concepts that we find useful.

We know, or presume, that our thoughts create our destiny. We therefore want to think positively, lovingly, and constructively. However, if we tell ourselves that we are healthy, happy, content, strong, balanced, etc., while feeling the opposite, we accomplish nothing. Our predominant thought pattern becomes one of lack as we compare our affirmative thoughts to what is "really going on." There is a feeling of having to work hard at "selling ourselves."

Keep it simple. Create a simple mantra: "health." What does your subconscious have to question? There is little room for doubt: just one simple word.

"And—?" your subconscious may ask.

"No 'and,'" you answer calmly.

Truthfully, this is a brilliant trick to outsmart the subconscious, with all its doubts and fears. As long as you think only the word "health" without any conditions attached to it like "I want . . . I must . . . I need . . . I do not have . . ." your subconscious has nothing to nag you about. One little word can have a powerful effect on your insides. Now, consider what one little word like "illness" or "failure" can do to you.

It is best to think only of words that give you a positive feeling. In this way, you can reprogram your subconscious. If no doubts are activated, the subconscious relaxes. It does nothing but listen, absorb, and translate.

Maybe, for years you have thought: "I am healthy, I am healthy," but underlying this is the core belief "I have never been healthy, and besides, this technique can't work for me anyway."

Now, instead, you merely sit comfortably and think only of concepts that make you happy, such as: beautiful flowers, meadows, mountains, sunshine, vacations, love, health, many friends, affectionate contact, etc. You can think of such concepts for hours and, not once, will your subconscious object because you are merely creating a gentle mental picture. You are not demanding: "Subconscious, do this, don't think that!" You are merely formulating concepts with no attachment. The good news is that these concepts seep even more deeply into your subconscious because there is no resistance, and like a computer, your brain will retain whatever is "saved" for future use. (Garbage in, garbage out, or in this case: beauty in, beauty out.)

With practice, you may build up sufficient confidence to try your hand at complete sentences. But, beware: the trick here, is to think of only those things in which you have complete confidence. If you have less than a thousand dollars in your bank account, you should never think: "I am rich" or even "I will be rich." However, sentences, such as: "I like wealth," "I find abundance fulfilling," or "I love living a life of wealth," are most effective. They do not give the subconscious anything to question. Interestingly, by doing this, you may also discover that saying "I like wealth" is uncomfortable because it is not really true. All the better. Now, you have the awareness to discover what you do like.

Starting a sentence with "I like _____" or "I love _____" is always good, filling in the blank with whatever it is that you desire. If you say to yourself, for example: "I love a big garden," your subconscious has nothing to criticize. The only thing it has to go on is: "My boss [meaning *you*] loves a big garden. I can see this garden. Fine." The subconscious remains at ease with this image, processing at its own speed.

This creates a very different response than the thought: "I have a big garden," when the reality is that you do not. Your underlying logic "knows better," and the contradiction causes stress on the system. (Unless you belong to that rare breed of happy people, capable of conceiving such a thought in childlike innocence, devoid of any sense of indignant lack.)

Even the thought: "I will get a big garden soon" opens the door for questions like "Oh, but how could this happen?" Only the statement "I love a big garden" contains nothing to provoke doubt. It therefore has the greatest chance of being manifested.

You can repeat such a sentence often, programming your whole system gently and slowly without exerting pressure, without giving your subconscious any stressful commands.

When I place an order with the universe, I do the opposite: I state my desire only once. However, in that case, it is necessary to release the order and forget about it, sending it forth with childlike trust. Otherwise, it rarely works.

For those orders you have made with the universe that have not yet worked, medi-playing is the perfect alternative. You can say the concepts to yourself as often as you like. You don't have to apply any trick in order to forget about your desire, and if you keep it simple, doubts will not arise.

The single catch is that you usually must wait longer for the changes to occur in your life. They are usually sneaky and will surprise you. It is always a revelation how many tiny sunbeams crawl slowly through the back door, lighting an entire room.

Medi-playing is also dynamic and interactive, responding best to those words or sentences towards which you feel the most affinity at the moment. Therefore, each time you medi-play (a twenty-minute session is optimal), you should focus on concepts that are particularly meaningful to you that day. In this way, the game will remain vibrant and consequently extremely effective.

Every day, new things happen, and every day, new concepts become meaningful to you. For example, after a particularly stressful day at the office, relaxation with good-natured people becomes most important to you. You may affirm: "I love quiet time with open landscapes and happy, carefree people in a vacation mood."

Do you see where the trick lies? You give yourself everything that you lacked that day, without the pressure of having "to do" anything.

Actually, this technique is the direct opposite of cosmic ordering, but nonetheless, I feel it has a place in this book because it proves the point: match your technique to your life. Absorb everything that you find beneficial, without questioning the source, and your inner power will increase automatically.

*Rule 6*: Observe your inside. This is analogous to following the pendulum of an old grandfather clock with your gaze: it is difficult to see slight variations unless you really look. You should think your word or your sentence once and then look inside, observing your body. How does the concept feel? Are there any reactions in the stomach, in the chest, in the solar-plexus, in the big toe, in the ears?

Wallow in the observation of your body. The pendulum swings in one direction and you think: "In everything, I see the miracle of life." The pendulum goes in the other direction, and somewhere in your body something relaxes. Then, you think the same sentence again or create a new one, searching for the trigger of your most intense feelings. This is the whole technique. With this, you cannot go wrong.

If you would like to take me up on my initial playful suggestion of turning my rules upside down, then get ready for the "anti-rules!" It is actually a good idea to experiment with the anti-rules. You may encounter surprising results. Even if your outcome is dreadful, that can only reinforce your commitment to the medi-play rules the next time. Your heightened confidence will make the game even more effective.

*The anti-rules:*

*Rule 1:* Sit upright with your back perfectly straight.

*Rule 2:* During the course of the meditation, do not move for any reason.

*Rule 3:* Play meditative music or sounds.

*Rule 4:* Think of nothing.

*Summary of medi-playing:*

*Rule 1:* Sit comfortably.

*Rule 2:* Moving is allowed.

*Rule 3:* Silence is best. No music.

*Rule 4:* Thoughts are allowed.

*Rule 5:* Think of words or sentences that one views as the most positive and constructive at the moment. The sentences should contain nothing that must be attained but only consist of positive observations that can be imagined and felt: "I like this," "I love that," or "I find X and Y beautiful." This does not provoke our subconscious doubts.

*Rule 6*: Allow the sentence or the word to have an effect on the body and observe how it feels.

An easy modification of this method is the gratitude technique. You think, each morning, of everything for which you are presently grateful—or for which you could be grateful. At first, it may be difficult to think of anything. This does not matter. With practice, the thoughts will come. Start simply. On the first morning, your thoughts of gratitude could go something like this:

I am grateful that there is still enough toothpaste, so I don't need to buy it.

I am grateful that I have a roof over my head.

I am grateful that I was not born in the desert.

I am grateful that I don't have any green curls.

This sounds like slight gratitude, but gratitude—like everything else—attracts more of the same, so even slight gratitude attracts more things for which to be grateful. Before you know it, so many good things will have come into your life that you can't help but say: "I am simply grateful for everything, for it would take the entire day to name individually all the wonderful things in my life!"

One final hint: these techniques will not lose their effectiveness simply because you do not dutifully devote yourself to them on a regular basis. Even if you remember to practice only once a month—and really badly at that—you can still benefit from the gratitude technique or medi-playing. They both work marvelously in single-application doses!

Certainly, it is probably true that the long-term effects will be better if you apply the techniques consistently—say, twice daily for twenty minutes at a time. But only then, if you do it with joy. My suggestion is this: submit to the discipline only if you see sufficient benefit to warrant such daily exercise. Follow your own sense of well-being.

# Love and Hate Are
# Two Sides of the Same Coin

Can you imagine that the people you hate, are actually the people you love? (If you hate anyone, that is.) Terrifying thought, except . . . it seems perfectly logical that we simply overlook people with whom we feel no connection. We do not even notice they are there. Whenever someone strikes us—whether positively or negatively—he or she has meaning in our lives. Behind all things, which somehow excite our special attention, a gift hides itself. We must only claim it.

With the following report of *Familienaufstellung*, or "family-installation therapy" (a psychotherapeutic procedure adapted by Bert Hellinger), I hope to inspire you to seek a greater understanding of this dynamic in your own life. Who is most noticeable to you in your own life? Have you uncovered the gifts hidden within this relationship?

Below, I am citing the article, "The Therapeutic Miracle: Family Installations," that I originally wrote for my magazine, *Solar Wind*, because it so clearly illustrates how love and hate intertwine and how our souls recognize only absolute value—not distinctions of "positive" or "negative."

With the worldwide need of personality development on the increase, therapy forms, themselves, are changing. They are becoming simpler, more intelligent, and more effective, occurring on a level where the esoteric and the commonplace come together. One only needs to approach the essence of life to discover that, in the final analysis, everyone speaks the same language. This, for me, is what is most fascinating about family installations: the way they expand the abilities of discernment, without restriction, for all humans. This cannot be called clairvoyance as it works for everyone!

*We must listen to our soul*
*if we wish to become healthy!*
*In the end, we are here*
*because there is no escape.*
*As long as one does not meet himself*
*in the eyes and heart*
*of his fellow man,*
*he is running away.*
*As long as he does not admit to his fellow man*
*what is in his heart,*
*he will not find security.*
*As long as he is afraid*
*to be penetrated,*
*he can never recognize himself—he will be alone.*

—Hildegard von Bingen

The term "family installations" had come up many times in my social circle. Everyone seemed to attend, and all returned inspired. Nonetheless, it really held no interest for me. Despite the fact that it consisted of a mere four days of group work, it was still a type of therapy, and therapy did not interest me at the time.

However, I also realized that I was storing "family karma" in my cellular memory and would need to release this in order to be completely free.

I wanted to be "Unchained from Destiny" (the title of one of my favorite songs, released by the group The Chains of Fate), yet I felt that no one really needed therapy. Utter nonsense.

Then, a series of events transpired in my life that reminded me of a funny, yet poignant, parable:

There is a huge flood, and a man sits on his roof because the rest of his house is already under water. The man prays to God that his life may be spared. Shortly thereafter, a boat passes by and offers to take the man on board. He refuses, saying he has faith that God will save him. And so, he remains on the roof. The man continues to pray, and two more boats pass by. However, the man remains on his roof, continuing his prayers. The water level rises higher and higher, and finally, the man drowns.

Arriving in heaven, he says to God: "I prayed fervently for your help! Why didn't you do anything to save me?"

God replies in bewilderment: "What do you mean? I sent three boats to you!"

I seemed to be operating under a similar misconception in my own life, holding stubbornly to my own view of the way my orders "should" be fulfilled. While I was drowning in my own sea of negative family karma, a series of boats (i.e., the references to family-installation therapy) sailed so closely by I could have touched them. But I wanted nothing to do with boats. I had my own idea of how I should be saved.

How often do the greatest gifts of life hide behind those things that one rejects?

My inner voice picked up on my ambivalence: "It is true: many times, a new concept has been presented to you, which you have been reluctant to try. When you finally do get around to it, you are often amazed at its simplicity and power. Meanwhile, you have wasted considerable time and energy grappling with yourself. Why not save yourself from this silly game of tug-of-war? Why not find out, once and for all, if anything lies behind this family-installation therapy? You know you are intrigued by it!"

Okay, I got the point. When something holds no meaning for me, I feel nothing. My feelings of strong dislike for the therapy probably meant that it resonated with me in some way. Ah, love and hate: opposite sides of the same coin!

I found the addresses of several different therapists and announced to myself that I would go to whoever had the first available opening.

Now, I must translate the experience of these four days into words. Unfortunately, in so doing, I can only recreate a small fraction of what transpired, for one must truly experience it.

There were twenty-five of us, between the ages of twenty-two and seventy. A few were of a particularly spiritual nature, but most seemed to be completely normal "average people" with minimal knowledge of things spiritual.

We went around the room, stating our first name, our occupation, and what we were trying to accomplish by being here. Then, the first installation began. It was completely voluntary. One came forward when—and if—he or she had the feeling to do so.

The installations functioned in such a way that one sat down on the "hot seat" beside the therapists and briefly stated his/her unresolved issue, such as: a strained relationship in the original family (parents, brothers and sisters, etc.) or problems in the current family/relationship etc. Interpretations of who did what or why were unimportant. What mattered were cold, hard facts. Also, the deceased or so-called prodigal loved ones could play a role.

The therapist projected himself into the energy of the person and thus decided with whom to begin. Then, the subject rose and found, from the group, someone to play the father, someone to play the mother, people to represent brothers and sisters, and even, a representative of the subject himself. The subject appointed the representatives by touching them on the shoulder, transferring the bonding energy. Completely unique constellations thusly emerged.

Sometimes, the installed family members looked at each other; sometimes, they stood with their backs to one another; sometimes, they hovered together; sometimes, they sat very far apart. Each installation took on its own character as the participants projected themselves into their new roles, observing what feelings arose from the process. The therapist asked everyone how they felt in their current position. Nothing more.

This is the part that caused me the most fear because I was unable to tune into how I was really feeling. "Perhaps, I lack the sixth sense, after all," I thought. What happened then, however, was simply brilliant, proving, yet again, the unfathomable ingenuity of the universe, which contains all things in the simplest detail.

When one sits for the first time in such an installation, she knows nothing about the strange family that has just developed; however, because there are so few environmental influences, because one actually does know nothing at all, because thinking is not sensing, one's perceptions slow down and become more acute.

For example, I could stand far away from everyone with my back toward them. The therapist asks me how I am. The answer is simple: I am as I am. It could be "good" or "bad." Sometimes, I might stand there, feeling completely stable; sometimes, I might have trouble breathing. Some people in the installation do not interest me; some say nothing to me. A higher mechanism intervenes to help one slip into the role that represents the person in the hot seat. One simply becomes this person, without having to act it, feeling everything the subject feels.

In the first installation, I was chosen to represent the subject. Suddenly, I became so sad that I was moved to tears. My mind immediately tried to make me feel embarrassed, telling me that I was not normal, that I must really be in need of therapy if I could lose control of my emotions in front of all these unfamiliar people.

It turned out that the person whom I represented felt neglected and overlooked and was quite sad about it. As my neighbor suddenly noticed me, taking me in from head to toe, something strange happened. As suddenly as the sorrow had come over me, there came instead, a sense of calmness and comfort. The longer my neighbor looked at me, and the more openly and intensely he looked, the more blissful I felt. At last, someone was acknowledging my existence! There was no doubt about what I was feeling.

In retrospect, I can say that my own installation was only a small part of the whole experience. I drew just as much from participating in the installation of others, so equally did I comprehend the root of their feelings. It seemed to work for everyone in this way. The twenty-two-year-old filled the role of grandfather just as well as the seventy-year-old did. The seventy-year-old seemed as comfortable as the twenty-two-year-old becoming the rebellious son. These installations reduce life to such basic elements that no one can miss it. In addition, the air of casualness that our therapist spread made us feel that nothing strange was going on at all. This influenced everyone without exception.

In another installation, I was the eighteen-year-old daughter, product of a first marriage, who lived with her father, his second wife, and their four-year-old son. I felt peevish in this role and had no desire to open up emotionally. I hated my half-brother, while, for my stepmother, I was unable to feel anything. She did not interest me.

In step two of the installation process, the picture is changed. One surveys the situation and decides in whose shoes he/she would like to stand in order to recognize what must be clarified or altered in the relationships. Through "healing words" that the therapist introduces and the subject repeats, and through healing images, the situation is altered from the inside. In the final analysis, it all depends on this. The outward situation can be however one truly desires it to be. The way one feels inside is what counts.

In the case of my mirroring the daughter of the first marriage, the father (who was the subject or the "installer," if you will) clarified his relationship with his first wife. We simply reenacted the scenario, which naturally occurred from our installation, and the therapist prompted his feelings as if it were "really" happening to him. Again, I was amazed at how genuinely I embodied the daughter's role. As "my parents" came to terms with their relationship, I immediately began to like my half-brother and became curious about my stepmother, even feeling joy at the prospect of properly getting to know her for the first time. The picture of peace between my birth parents made this possible.

The father's second wife was actually present and played herself. I had the feeling that she was also relieved that the situation with the first wife had been clarified and that she sensed how much this did for the emotional health of the daughter.

Now, the critical mind will object: "Yes, well, that is all fine, but in *reality*, the people involved are still in conflict. What use is such a pretend family?"

Again, this is an intangible that one simply has to experience in order to believe it. Words, here, are completely inadequate; however, I will attempt to recreate the essence through three primary points:

First of all, exterior life circumstances are much less important than we think. Our internal images and feelings are what truly matter. I can correct these, converting them from damaging to healing, even if the people involved are dead or far away.

There was a woman in our group who, at the age of two, had witnessed the murder of her mother. Even in such an extreme situation, the correct picture to heal the inside can develop from installation therapy.

Secondly, we are all energetically connected. The soul of another alters if I change my internal image of him or her. A single mother experienced this after her installation, in which the father of her child suddenly perceived the desire to take more responsibility for their child—something she had not been willing to ask of him. She also recognized that her child would grow up, not only without a father, but with a feeling of unworthiness, if she did not change her attitude: whenever she looked at her child, she saw, at least unconsciously, her ex-partner. This filled the woman with contempt and fury. As the result, the child could not help but feel rejected.

Through the installation, the woman can re-experience the man as a human being to be respected, simply as the father of her child—regardless of what was or is. If she regards the aspects of the man that are present in her child with this feeling of respect, then the child is energetically interconnected in love with his father and really does not grow up without him, even if the father is physically absent. One must feel the difference. One simply must experience such an installation. It cannot be understood by the head, only by the heart.

Thirdly, with such a four-day enclosure, one develops a new sense of reality and what is truly important. Admittedly, I already understood intellectually that the people we hate the most are the ones we actually love the most. However, I did not "know" it on a soul level until I had experienced family-installation therapy. It is one thing to comprehend a concept; it is quite another to experience how rapidly feelings can change when one sits in the position of installer and disseminates the problem.

The soul perceives only the extent of the contribution; it has no interest in reading plus or minus signs. It does not perceive those it does not love. It overlooks them dispassionately. Everyone knows this feeling. On the other hand, the soul often attracts people to itself that trigger fear or fury.

Then, there are others that cause the soul no harm, but they are of no significance. The soul does not respond, moving on from these people without developing any emotions toward them.

As a result of the therapy, my soul communicated to me that it feels strongly for some humans, while for others, it feels no resonance. If the people, whom I love, are not in harmony, I feel pain. If the pain becomes too great, I perceive it as anger.

The bottom line: what the soul finds important is not who gave me life (i.e. my parents) or how my parents live or why they left. I hate those people for whom the feeling of love would be too painful. (Perhaps, my father was an aggressive alcoholic who beat my mother.) During the installation, my soul zeros in on whatever my true feelings are. If someone yells at me daily, causing me anguish, perhaps that is a good reason to stay away from him. However, during an installation, I can experience the love hidden behind the anger. I can heal my inner image, allowing myself to sense what the contribution of this person—even if it instills fury—truly means in the end.

By feeling the essence behind this experience, I heal myself. I take the first step in changing my reality. As long as I live in fear, never looking behind the old pictures of my mind, my life will not change. I am the only one who can change me.

# Coincidence versus Providence

Whoever studies mental laws, his own thoughts, or how his attitudes—and those of others—shape the world we live in determines, sooner or later, that strange "coincidences" and unlikely divine providences occur increasingly often. If one brings up the subject of such uncanny occurrences, one is likely to receive one of two standard answers. The first one is: "Nope, I have never experienced such things. They are not real. Such nonsense!"

Answer number two: "Ah, yes, I am where I am today as a result of such coincidences." Some even add: "I consider these coincidences to be a sign, whether something is in harmony with the divine will or not. Most of the moves I make depend on such coincidences. Life is too exhausting otherwise."

In order to illustrate what is possible, I have included two coincidences or providences that actually transpired: one was of a physical nature, the other, spiritual. These coincidence experiences—told from the points of view of Manfred and Franz, respectively—show to what extent the universe will go to bring us to our true joy. Hopefully, from the example of these first-person accounts, you can determine whether or not you are, as of yet, "sucking the marrow" of everything the universe has to offer.

*Situation number 1: Manfred, a 60-year-old micro-photographer, through coincidence, turned into a castle-owner.* It all started with two musicians who played synthesizers. They looked a bit scraggly, but I admired them at that time. It was only later that I learned they were dealing hashish. Essentially, they financed their music from the money earned by selling drugs. As I said, at least at that time, this was unknown to me—although one of them was already being legally detained. He was quite a well-known artist, but he was somewhat crazy. For example, he had the insane idea to pack the air of Berlin in tin cans and to sell real "Berlin air." He opened the cans, really "locked in" pure West Berlin air, and sold them everywhere.

In any event, he and his friend had searched for an area where they could make music undisturbed. They had come up with the idea to rent a castle. No sooner had they made an appointment for the first phase of negotiations with Count Rechberg—or rather, his architect—when one of the potential castle dwellers was taken into custody. They couldn't go, of course, so they sent me instead.

I, Manfred, did them a favor and met with the architect, posing as the potential tenant. This architect immediately asked me a thousand questions, such as: "What do you do?" "Why, then, do you want a castle?" "What do you imagine the castle should look like?"

At first, I was startled. Not having given the matter much thought, I was completely unprepared. So, I imagined:

"what if?" From this, I was able to improvise an entirely new scenario of why I searched for a castle if I were, in fact, searching for one. In the most colorful detail, I presented him with my reasons, even making up the perfect size castle to match my situation and my institute, which I had in reality. I began with my real-life situation and stretched an imaginary story around it to explain why I would look for a castle.

I must have sounded sufficiently plausible, for I was given the keys to the castle, which I could visit anytime. Soon afterward, my wife and I took a look around. It was not feasible—either for my fictional situation or for the real-life situation of the musicians—at least, not according to what I knew. The castle consisted of five individual buildings, which were all impractical. In addition, they were quite dilapidated. Horse stables and cow stalls were also included, which none of us needed. We therefore returned to the architect, expressing disinterest.

"Well," he said, handing us another set of keys. "Perhaps White-Stone would better suit you."

My wife and I didn't have anything better to do, so we took a drive to see the second castle. My wife was immediately aflame with ideas of where everything could go: the kitchen, my laboratory, guest rooms, etc. She carefully divided up the total area, in her imagination, to serve our every possible need. I also toyed gladly with these ideas, of course: an imaginary trip where one enters a new, imaginary country. And so, we passed through sixty-three rooms, integrating them together with our plans, considering the castle despite its run-down condition.

Then, we returned to the architect. "So, what do you think?" he asked. I repeated the same objections I had used on the first castle, but my wife began to rave about how this castle was exactly right: the size was perfect, the various wings were interconnected (unlike the first castle), etc. It could be just as we imagined. Without a single doubt, she could move into such a castle. Her enthusiasm was catching, and I said: "It is certainly to be considered; however, the roof is in terrible disrepair and must be replaced. . . ." I added several other conditions to my list.

The architect was undisturbed; he was fully aware of the condition of the castle. "The owner does not wish to repair these things unless someone shows serious interest," he replied.

I dutifully turned over a file of my qualifications, including some magazine feature articles on me, which had contributed greatly to my reputation. In short, I did everything I could to secure the renting of a castle for my musician friends.

However, then it happened. One week later, our second house, which we were renting for my institute, was abruptly sold. Our residence, which belonged to my wife, afforded limited space. The second house had sixteen large rooms, providing sufficient space for my entire institute. It had been used as a warehouse and belonged to the mail service. They were dumping it in a short-term sale, and I had to vacate. The house was located very favorably near our residence. I only needed to walk across the yard.

I started to look everywhere for a substitute location for my institute. As of yet, I had not fully gestated the lunatic idea of renting—or even buying—the castle; so I continued to search for another house situated near our residence. A long, fruitless search followed, which fed my despair. What should I do?

One week later, the architect called. He had shown my records to Count Rechberg, the owner of the castle, who had agreed that I could have White-Stone. At first, I was speechless. In the midst of my current problem, I had given no further thought to the castle.

Nonetheless, I paid another visit to White-Stone and discussed my situation with the architect. "What, then, can you afford to pay?" He wanted to know. He discussed market conditions for rentals and introduced a whopping figure of $6,000 a month.

"That is completely impossible," I replied. "I now pay $4,800 for the entire YEAR!" The most I could possibly afford for the rental was about $2,500 a month.

"Of course," offered the architect. "You could also buy it! Confidentially, I can tell you that the count would like to get $400,000 for the castle; however, he knows it is in a desolate condition. To be able to sell it at all, he would have to invest close to $250,000 in repairs to bring it up to code. The count has been looking for a buyer for four years, but he is selective: he wants someone who will respect the property and not tarnish its reputation. Thanks to these ideals, he has become increasingly enslaved to the estate over time. In addition, a few prospects who were 'worthy' insisted that the repairs be completed before they took possession. . . . What if the count deducted the $250,000 he would spend in repairs from the sale price? You could have the castle 'as is' for $150,000."

This sounded like a good deal, but I still needed to figure out how I would raise the $150,000! I then went to my musician friends with the information. To my surprise, they wanted nothing more to do with it. All they had wanted, they told me, was a place to practice undisturbed for about $1,000 per month. They realized it had been a crazy idea, after all.

Well, I took the crazy idea home to my wife. For the first time, we seriously considered buying the place. However, it did not take long for us to consider: "Now that we know it is possible to own a castle, why settle for this one? Let us see what else is out there." And so, we spent the next two weeks castle hunting.

We looked at everything from palaces with golden faucets, renting for $10,000 per month, to ruins for no rent at all that could be acquired by signing a renovation agreement. At the end of those two weeks, we knew that White-Stone was our favorite castle and the most suitable for both the institute and our living quarters. We were still not certain, however, if Count Rechberg would agree to sell the property for $150,000.

Another two weeks passed, and the architect called again. Count Rechberg was in agreement. Unbelievable!

Then, the money search began in earnest. I scratched and sniffed in all corners. Fortunately, the first third of the money came from a large order that mysteriously appeared. Then, some overseas accounts that had been waiting for authorization finally cleared. A series of coincidences seemed to contribute further monies to the cause. Nonetheless, we were still $30,000 short. Then, my wife remembered her deceased mother's savings accounts, which she had not yet touched out of piety. And how much was in the account? Exactly $30,000!

I consolidated our resources and presented Count Rechberg with a check, in the amount of $150,000. Now, we owned the castle outright!

Next, I went to a bank to borrow money for the repairs. We had needed to raise the $150,000 because we did not have sufficient collateral. However, the outright ownership of a castle altered the picture: "You need a loan? No problem. How much?"

My wife oversaw the repairs, and we moved in two months later. That was twenty-five years ago, and we are still the proud owners of a castle. It all began with a fabrication: what requirements would a castle need to meet if I, in fact, were looking for one? It was as if my mental construct became a runaway train that I could not exit. The story had a momentum all its own, and its energy attracted all subsequent events that led to such a perfect outcome.

I stood there with the architect, literally inventing the reasons why I wanted a castle. Intellectually, I was operating under the premise: what would I do if my second house were no longer available to me? Little did I know that reality was a mere eight days away! Can that be coincidence?

My wife and I never would have gotten the idea to rent a castle with sixty-three rooms, let alone *buy* one if I had not been forced to vacate the second house. The whole idea was, indeed, crazy. But now, I have owned this castle for years, and it fits our lives perfectly. It simply had to be so!

*Situation number 2: Franz, a forty-year-old electrical engineer, has a metaphysical experience in Caracas.* I had recently turned forty and had worked for one year in Caracas, during which time I had lived apart from my wife, Inge. Before I had taken the job, our relationship had already been on the rocks. I had hoped that our marriage would sort itself out again someday, somehow. Inge and our daughter, Linda, had recently returned home to Germany after spending a vacation with me in Caracas. During their stay, Inge had informed me that she wanted to end our marriage to marry another man. And so, I sat, writing a letter to my wife.

*Dear Inge* was all I had written. The attempt to formulate even the first sentence had filled me with despair. The realization of my utter impotence, that there was no sentence that could alter the situation, paralyzed me. I believed in God, so I prayed—or rather, begged—that he might intervene.

By chance, the lamp suddenly, softly, went out. This startled me because my thoughts and the small blackout were so synchronistic. I changed the bulb, but the lamp went out again. A strange feeling came over me. I was extremely willing, in my current condition, to experience a miracle, but this was only a normal power failure. I was simply reading more into it, due to my state of mind. Or maybe not. Could it be a sign?

I had hardly asked myself that question when the lamp came on and went out—three times in a row! That was enough. I should not be so bold as to expect more "signs," I thought. Goose bumps overtook my body from head to toe. I decided to admit that whatever "it" was, this was definitely "it."

If a miracle wanted to occur, it should just do it; however nothing more happened. What should one do upon receiving a sign from above? I had no idea. Finally, I turned off the lamp and went to bed, concentrating on being open to receive something from somewhere.

An awareness slowly came over me. I could even determine from where it came: there was a presence behind the door, leading into the kitchen. The presence was not visible, but it existed all the same. The hairs at the back of my neck stood on end. "Stop," I said to myself. "This is utter non-sense. Seven times three equals twenty-one. What did I watch on television yesterday? What needs to be done at work tomorrow? I left those boys with a transistor-intensifier; they always have fun with those . . . Ah, no, that thing is still there!" The feeling was too strong to be ignored.

Okay, there is an invisible presence behind the door. It is watching me, and it is not going away. Why should I not accept it? After all, I liked uncommon things. "Very well," I said. "I accept that you are here. No doubt, you are here because you want something: that is logical. Therefore, come on out! I am ready."

The presence obliged, approaching slowly. Shivers ran down my spine. It was two meters away, then one. I was consumed by fear, but I remained still. It came nearer and nearer. Then, it touched me. My fear vanished. With my eyes closed, I saw into a man's face: approximately thirty-five-years old, short curls, blond, friendly. He was agreeable, and he had a relaxing effect on me. "Who are you?" I asked, but received no response.

The man turned away his face and slowly disappeared. Although the distance between him and me increased, I was able to see more of his shape: he wore a white cloak.

What did this mean? A presence appeared and then vanished? "Come back and tell me what you want!" I called to him in thought. It worked. He returned, as softly as before. However, this time, he was more than just a notion. This time, I had no fear; in fact, quite the opposite. With joy, I transmitted the thought that I was receptive. Promptly, something approached me. Seconds seemed like hours before the touch. With that touch, I expected to see his face again, but this time, it was different. I saw nothing; instead, I felt my daughter, Linda.

It was the most astonishing thing, the way I "felt" her. I could not sense, hear, or see her: I had become her. A few seconds later, as Linda, I was at home, in Germany, lying in bed. Then, I became myself again, lying in the bed in Caracas. There were some more comings and goings that my spirit was not fully able to absorb. Each time that I realized I was Linda, my logical mind complained and brought me back to myself again.

Then, I had a blackout: Linda departed from my consciousness. My equilibrium was overburdened trying to readjust after the experience, and I felt sick. I needed help, and it came: my spirit or soul or whatever represented my higher self climbed higher and higher, stopping only when the Earth could be perceived as a ball below. I was over the Atlantic Ocean, in the middle of Europe and South America, with a clear view of both Venezuela and Germany. Linda was beside me. I could no longer sense her thoughts, but I could see her. It was beautiful to be so high above. I first showed Germany to Linda with outstretched arm, where her body now had to be, and then Venezuela. I talked insistently to her, how I would do well by her; however, the vision slowly lost strength. Finally, I found myself in my own bed, alone.

Well, what should I make of that? With every minute that removed me from the experience, I became more certain that I had imagined it all. I simply didn't believe it. After the blackout, everything had only happened in my head. I went to sleep.

A few days passed, and the incident with Linda lost importance. However, somehow, I was feeling better. No longer was I filled with self-pity. One evening, I had a long telephone conversation with Inge, during which she informed me that Linda had become ill shortly after returning home from their trip to see me. She had suffered from fevers and extreme fatigue. Two doctors had been unable to determine the cause.

The third, however, suggested that Linda's expectation had obviously been that her father would return home with the family after the vacation. The bitter disappointment of this not coming to pass could have triggered indefinable, psychosomatic illness.

Then, one night, Linda had had a vision: she had been high above the ocean! I had been with her and had showed her Germany and Venezuela. Linda's health returned the following morning.

I was overjoyed. I had experienced something miraculous, and it had been real! It had been a kind of telepathy, confirmed by the other side, which had even had a direct effect on Linda's health. The presence that had first appeared to me had acted as a mediator, making the mental connection possible. Had it also caused the blackout?

The experience had revealed a new world to me, beyond the physical surface of nature. Unequivocally, there was a reality outside our everyday perceptions, in which beings of a non-material nature existed. These beings had abilities nearly beyond our comprehension. The Western religions call these beings "angels." In any event, the experience was wonderful, and I wanted to experience something similar again.

Several days later, I noticed a poster: "First International Convention of Parapsychology in Caracas." I took time off from work to attend the convention. There were many interesting accounts, but the demonstrations were disappointing.

Neither the self-professed healers, nor the mind readers were successful. Nonetheless, I did meet the director, who was a mnemonics instructor. She had organized the *Venezuelan Institute for Parapsychology*, which offered instructional seminars in parapsychology. I signed up.

To me, the seminar seemed like a group of people questing after otherworldly powers. It, too, was disappointing. None of the experiments worked: no pendulums moved, no insights automatically came through the pencil, no matches spontaneously ignited through the power of a stiff gaze. At the end of ten weeks, we received diplomas that read: "Citizen of the Universe." We had been transformed!

In all seriousness, there had been a small change. I began to be viewed by people, both privately and at work, as an expert in parapsychology. This is how I met my friend, Luis, for example. As a side business during the evening hours, we developed a car alarm system, which we then sold.

I grew to like Luis very much. I admired how well he got along with his wife, child, and in-laws; how seriously he took his job; how efficiently he repaired cars; how he used his electronics knowledge to earn extra money.

Well, the situation that ignited our friendship was a coincidence in and of itself! One day, Luis ran through the laboratory in a strangely bent position, complaining to me of his misery. That morning, while beginning work on a heavy electric motor, an intense pain had shot through him. Since then, he had been unable to stand up straight.

In the break room, over coffee and cigarettes, he asked me about parapsychology: "Surely, at that seminar, you learned something about the laying on of hands?" Luis inquired, in the hopes that I could heal his back.

Not taking myself too seriously, I ran my right hand—while still holding a cigarette—along his back. "Luis, whether you believe it or not, I sense exactly where it hurts you," I said. In amazement, I discarded my cigarette and examined Luis' back. Moving my right hand barely two inches down his back, I felt a strange sensation, like a small, repelling magnet field. I quite clearly sensed it in my hand: I had no need to touch—let alone—probe his flesh.

"And I sense exactly where your hand is," Luis replied. "Keep going: you're doing good work!"

After about a minute, Luis stretched and beamed: he was free from pain and could continue as before.

The cure of Luis and the incident with Linda marked the beginning of a whole series of cures, as well as other uncommon events, that I was able to manifest. Had that spiritual presence transferred special abilities to me through his touch?

To be sure, I carried out a whole series of experiments. Some succeeded; some did not. In particular, I practiced the laying on of hands because I could not figure out why it sometimes worked so wonderfully for me, while other times, it failed. Clearly, there was a force outside of human influence directing this process. It was also clear that I was being directed. Why, then, was I not simply directed to those with whom I had the greatest chance for success? "Why can't I receive a sign?" I asked the universe.

One day at lunch break, I was sitting at the canteen with a full cup of coffee. One of the technicians, who serviced the radio equipment, entered. At this precise moment, I knocked over my coffee. I had the strange sensation that a foreign influence had taken over my actions. Of my own volition, I would never have knocked over the coffee. I sensed that something was definitely not normal.

The technician came over to me and helped me clean the table. His shift would soon begin, shortly before mine ended. Another technician, with whom I was better acquainted, suddenly addressed me regarding the first man: "He has a bad toothache and still must work here the whole night. I have already told him about you. Please go to him and see what you can do."

I took him into a small adjacent room and immediately localized the sore tooth, removing the shooting pains simply by laying my hands across his energy field.

Subsequently, I encountered three more similar incidents. Always as a precursor, I knocked over my coffee cup when a certain person came into my proximity. Each time, it seemed to me like I had handed over the control of my body for a split second.

Eventually, the little routine with the coffee disappeared, only to be replaced by a series of other signs of an equally ordinary nature. Confidence in my own abilities certainly increased due to these experiences but so did my sense of responsibility.

One night, I dreamt that I was back in Germany, in my sister Karin's room. She complained because she was unable to listen to music: her stereo was broken. As an electronics expert, I started to dismantle it; however, I was unable to repair it. Finally, it was a relief just to succeed at putting everything back the way it had been. Karin simply said: "Let it be. Our brother Theo, has already tried to fix it."

I awakened suddenly, with the awareness that my sister was mentally ill. Naturally, I wanted to help by returning to Germany as soon as I could. Yet, the dream kept me away.

From it, I understood that I could be of no help to her, since I lacked the necessary knowledge or skill.

The next night, I dreamt again of Karin. We were in my grandmother's house, and Karin had packed her suitcases. I carried her suitcases into the car and drove with her to a big house where there were many people I had never seen before. She moved in there and said "goodbye" with eyes beaming. I asked her when she would return. She replied: "I will stay here." Then, I awoke.

The meaning of this dream became clear two months later when I flew to Germany for a short vacation. I visited my mother, with whom Karin lived at the time. She wasn't doing very well, but a doctor had found a place in a home for her. As it turned out, nobody had time to drive her there besides me.

Well, as of the present day, Karin has lived in the home, off and on, now, for ten years. She fares better at the home than she does anywhere else.

More recently, I was lying in bed but still awake. I sensed that a presence was approaching. Curiously, I sent my thoughts to the unknown being. As it came closer, I felt uneasy. Someone was terribly afraid. I could not see anything because the presence brought with it such darkness. Since I had experience with telepathy, I concentrated on breaking off the connection: everything was so black, and there was so much fear in this blackness. I sensed that the fear belonged to a person who needed help; however, that person remained in the blackness. I could find out no more. Therefore, I simply relaxed and tried to stand by the fear. This lasted approximately ten minutes before abruptly ending.

A few weeks later, the meaning became clear to me. Karin was at home, and she was not doing well. She had collapsed, remaining on the ground, powerless, for approximately ten minutes. It had been an extremely critical condition. She later told me that everything around her had gone black, and that she had been so afraid.

Well, all these coincidences have greatly influenced my life philosophy. I now experience a new kind of security. The universe has become a home in which I can thrive. I have discovered that something or somebody wonderful is most concerned about me and others. Even words have taken on an entirely new meaning: if I formulate a request or make a pronouncement, the response comes spontaneously, or at least, in a few days.

I have never learned who my spiritual guide or "guardian angel" is. This being never introduced himself to me before the telepathy experience with Linda. Who was it exactly? A living human with special powers? A being in an alternate state of consciousness?

When I discovered the laying on of hands, I had envisioned my source as Jesus. However, I do not know for certain. In the end, it does not matter, for the assistance has come.

Once, I thought that, perhaps, all deceased people form a common nature: one cannot speak to this nature as a whole but only to individual souls. These souls can then come to an agreement with the common nature about a certain wish. Consequently, this wish is realized. Nonetheless, this was just one of many theories that I devised to explain the phenomenon.

The problem with theories—and experiments—is that they may lead to a kind of spiritual burnout. One such burnout occurred surrounding my attempts to stop smoking. I wanted to stop because I knew that it would harm me in the long term. Besides, I was already going in the right direction: I smoked fairly innocuous cigarettes and no more than one pack a day. (There was a time when I had smoked two packs a day, unfiltered.) Since cigarettes were cheap in Venezuela, one could easily bum a smoke or two. So, my short-term goal was to buy no more cigarettes, limiting myself to smoking only what I could "scrounge." This worked for a while; then, I decided to stop completely.

I picked a deceased person from the aforementioned "common nature" to help me: John Lennon. I admired him, and, to me, he seemed sufficiently capable of this task. Therefore, I asked John Lennon to help me, promising that I would smoke no more. This lasted a few days, until finally, under stress, I placed a cigarette into my mouth. I only smoked for about five minutes before developing a sore throat. "John Lennon," I communicated via my thoughts, "I don't like this method one bit. I need help, not punishment." My protests were of no avail: I developed a cold.

While recovering, I abandoned the above model and modified my promise. My new promise was: I would not buy myself any more cigarettes, but if I could not keep this promise, it should not cost me my health. However, it could cost me financially. I put my car up for "collateral," so to speak. I also ordered that that the "reprimand" not be terribly expensive right away, and that it should be clear to me that it was "from above." That the universe would be *so* clear, however, I never would have dreamed.

Amazingly, I persevered for three weeks, sufficiently hitting up friends and colleagues so that I could still smoke about six to eight cigarettes per day. Then, one day, it was different. I had to drive alone to a radio station that was approximately two hours away from Caracas. Once there, I had to work alone, returning again in the afternoon. I had smoked nothing since the previous evening and would likely meet no one that I knew by the end of the day. The thought, alone, was unbearable.

On the return trip, I noticed an advertisement for cigarettes in front of a roadside stand, and I stopped.

What was my promise . . . just one pack? Not exactly. However, one simply cannot survive such promises!

I bought a pack of cigarettes and immediately had a smoke. I returned to my car and started the motor . . . or rather, I tried to start it . . .

A garage was right next door, and the repair cost approximately $100.00.

Over the next two months, I bought cigarettes three more times, and every time, the response "from above" came promptly. Each repair became somewhat more expensive. If I bought cigarettes, I had better do it next to a garage because it was obvious what would happen next. I accepted it, as I could not seem to stop it. I had to realize my weakness and live up to my promise. By the time I left Venezuela, I was still smoking about a half pack per day.

What should I now infer from all this? When I left Venezuela, I left parapsychology along with it, abandoning it for several years.

Eventually, though, I was reminded by two accidents that there is much more to the world than materialism and electronics. The renewal of my career as "master healer" was thanks to a woman named Mary, whom I freed of kidney stones in just one session.

Another spectacular cure occurred with my housekeeper's landlady. She had a strange, thick bump on her palm. Literally, within two minutes of laying my hands on her, the bump vanished completely.

At the time, these two experiences caused me to ponder where all this would lead. What I had channeled had been first-class miracles. If this got around, wouldn't people expect me to cure everything? Make the lame walk? Heal the blind to clear vision? Wouldn't people eventually expect me to explain these miracles, to share the wisdom? Ah, but a fool such as I simply had no idea at all! The only thing I had learned by the laying on of hands was to love everything that has life, from people to protozoa. That was my entire teaching.

Besides, I could be no saint. I loved women, group sex, and pornography. I also was not particularly courageous.

Today, I think that the so-called ESP capabilities are in everyone. How do you develop whatever ESP skill lies in you? I think you simply make it up! It is something you use daily without becoming conscious of it. Your subconscious has access to enormous strengths. In light of that fact, it would be wise to cultivate a harmonious relationship with it. Sometimes, it seems that your subconscious is your enemy. But that can never be, because it is a part of you.

It tries merely to alert you to your actual energies. Perhaps, you sometimes find it necessary to consciously discourage it by force. If this applies to you, no doubt, you would like to develop a more fruitful connection to your subconscious. How can this happen?

If you presume that your subconscious is constantly in action and handles unlimited strengths, the logical conclusion is that nothing which happens to you can be a coincidence. Every event that involves you, but in which you are not consciously involved, was caused by your subconscious.

Therefore, if you wish to better understand the conditions that befall you, you must better understand yourself. Don't force yourself to understand. Oftentimes, experiences link together like a puzzle, triggering understanding only through a key event. If you presume that there are no coincidences, that everything is caused by your subconscious, then your subconscious will become more receptive to you. In other words, it will thank you.

This is a simple way—unlike complex, experimental theories—that really works. You can bring together your consciousness and your subconscious, restoring yourself to wholeness. In this way, you can experience the abilities which were truly intended for you, and you will start to love yourself. With the ability to love yourself as a basis, you will be able to love each human being, for you will be able to see yourself in everyone. . . .

And so went the stories of Manfred and Franz: two very different men with very different experiences of "coincidence versus providence."

Keep in mind that the coincidences, themselves, did not increase the quality of these men's lives. The ability to recognize—and accept—the gifts offered by the universe are what made the difference.

# Tricks for Manifesting Miracles

In this chapter, I will show you why you should be happy if you are a novice, metaphysically speaking, and how to make the most of your status.

For one thing, surround yourself with your own kind: in other words, the metaphysically uninitiated, who have a critical advantage over the so-called "experts." The most productive inner attitude for manifesting miracles is that of an innocent child: ask without expectation and forget about it. Then, be gratefully amazed. This joyful humility is the fertile soil in which future miracles can grow.

It is the lack of this joyful humility that creates the biggest problems for the more experienced among us.

Here is an amusing, real-life example:

One of my best friends gave me the address of a clairvoyant, who is so good, her schedule is completely booked for over a year. Skeptics of the first degree go to her and come back believers.

The way the clairvoyant works is brilliant in its simplicity: the client sits on a chair without speaking, while the clairvoyant analyzes the client without asking a single question. The reading is so appropriate that one feels that all the pieces of his/her life have, at last, come together like a puzzle. One finally understands why situations are what they are and how they became that way.

Upon hearing this, I immediately think that it would be a good idea to send my Aunt Maryta to this clairvoyant. Trusting the universe, I know that no matter how long she has to wait for the appointment, it will be at the most appropriate time for her life situation.

When I pose all this to my aunt, she is quite taken with the idea and immediately calls the clairvoyant to reserve a date. Her appointment is set for two years in the future.

Time passes, and the date becomes imminent. Unfortunately, my aunt's most productive employee is going on vacation that same week, during which time several important deadlines must be met for an approaching sales event. Consequently, it would be difficult for her to justify missing work to keep an appointment with a clairvoyant!

On the other hand, when one waits so long for an appointment, its importance increases in one's mind, and it is difficult to simply dismiss it. As much as she wants to make that appointment, the sales event is rapidly approaching, squeezing her for time. Nothing in her store is ready, and she feels like she is running in circles, not knowing which way to turn or what to tackle first. The sale is opening that very weekend and includes a fashion show. Even if she cancels her appointment with the clairvoyant, she does not see how she can ever complete all the preparations in time. What should she do? She cannot bring herself to cancel the appointment.

One day before the appointment, the telephone in her store rings. There is a woman's voice on the other end. Apologizing profusely, the woman explains that the clairvoyant has been called away on an emergency and will be unable to keep their scheduled appointment. However, she could meet with Maryta in two weeks. Stunned, my aunt holds the receiver for a few moments: she is speechless. Nothing better could have happened! She is absolved! After recovering from her goose bumps, Maryta tells the lady what a miracle it is.

This experience calms her down so much that she is able to execute her work responsibilities with ease. Naturally, this ease transfers to the events themselves, and everything goes even better than planned. My aunt's inner reality of: "Well, if even *this* could be automatically resolved, then everything else can be, too" has lubricated the wheels of fortune—or coincidence.

This brings us to the point of experience versus inexperience. My aunt, who is still quite the novice in metaphysical matters, often doubts and dissects her perceptions. In this case, she is in such awe of the miracle that she cannot contain herself, and so, she immediately calls to tell me all about it, how fantastic it was, etc.

Niece Barbel, who has placated her questioning brain for many years with one metaphysical technique after the other, suppresses a yawn and announces soberly: "Beautiful. This obviously shows that you are operating in resonance with this woman's work, and the appointment in two weeks will be most worthwhile."

Cut. Next scene: two weeks later. Maryta's best employee has just returned from vacation, and Maryta tells her about the impending appointment with the clairvoyant.

Although the employee does not believe in such things, she has an adventurous spirit. So, she asks if she may come along. At this point, my aunt recounts the entire history leading up to the appointment. As she reaches the dramatic part, where her work responsibilities are closing in, forcing her to consider canceling the long-awaited appointment, the employee bursts out: "I know what happened next! The clairvoyant called to reschedule. Ha, ha! What a twist! Great story! The clairvoyant—being clairvoyant—was able to see that you didn't have the time. Ha, ha! That's a good one!" She doesn't believe a word.

Now, Aunt Maryta can tell wonderful jokes, which become even more effective because she is able to maintain both a serious tone and a straight face. Due to this skill, however, it is often difficult to determine whether she is being serious or not.

Nonetheless, the main reason the employee does not take the story seriously is that it seems much too incredible. To her way of thinking, it lies outside the realm of not only the probable, but also, the possible.

And so, once again, we arrive at the main point: to the employee, who is completely unschooled in spiritual matters, such an "ordinary" miracle is too mind-boggling to accept. She has the amazement of a small child, experiencing the world as something new, big, and unbelievable.

For the so-called "insiders," divine providences become commonplace. They are certainly joyful and "good" but no longer miraculous.

Whose orders is the universe most likely to grant—the person who takes the process for granted or the person who is wide-eyed with amazement?

It is akin to being in love. The first phase of amorousness makes one feel that being in love is the biggest miracle of all. Then, the phase of habituation comes on gradually, and the magic dissipates. Finally, the phase approaches in which one must consciously and intentionally recreate the relationship on a daily basis. All of a sudden, one must actually work at something (i.e. the relationship) that, at one time, seemed automatic.

Unfortunately, many other aspects of life work this way as well. As long as something is new, it can seem like a miracle, creating its own magnetic energy. However, as soon as that same thing becomes more familiar, the intoxication is no longer generated all by itself. One must place oneself in the rain, under the trees, and look upward into the treetop, quite consciously searching for that one, individual, miraculous drop. One can choose to see a heady and meditative experience in that drop, or one can simply say: "Oh, I'm wet. Hopefully, this will stop soon."

The childlike spirit reacts automatically, while the adult human being must decide consciously to rediscover the miracles of daily life. Just as one must rediscover his/her established relationships on a daily basis in order to appreciate them, one must constantly rediscover providences, so as not to become numb to them.

Whoever sends forth his orders to the universe full of awe at the miracles of creation has the best chance of success. However, whoever "places" his order in a bored mood of drudgery, approaching the matter as he would his tax return, will not fare so well.

How do you resuscitate your capacity for miracles once you have fallen into apathy? There are small, easy tricks for achieving this. The best ones are the ones you devise yourself.

Barring that, here are a few hints for reactivating your inner voice; in other words, here are a few tricks for manifesting miracles:

*Stage 1:* Sit down with your back straight and breathe naturally. For two minutes, tune into your solar plexus. How does it feel? Next, recall a situation that was especially pleasant for you. Relive all the details, such as: mood, smell, sound, thoughts, and feelings. How does your solar plexus feel now?

Now, recall one of the most unpleasant situations in your life. Once again, bring up all the details in your memory, allowing the situation to replay for you. How does your solar plexus feel now?

Return to your memory of the pleasant experience and impress it upon your mind. Tell yourself that, during the next unpleasant situation, you will immediately recall what a positive experience feels like.

If this practice works for you, you will make an exciting discovery: the moment you encounter an unpleasant situation, your recollections of the pleasant feeling in your solar plexus will gear your perception towards the trigger: an agreeable experience. Your solar plexus will automatically feel more open, receptive, and soft, altering the energy of the situation, itself.

Actually, you are harnessing your energy in the solar plexus in order to protect yourself from unpleasant impressions. Surprisingly, however, by doing this, you will determine that the unpleasant situation matters much less to you if you remain open and soft. The unpleasant energy merely passes through you, but it can do no harm, as it has nothing upon which to fasten itself.

Keep in mind that most of the behaviors you have developed, you have done so to protect yourself. However, at times of stress, your automatic reaction can be deceptive. Due to the strain, you may become open only to attack. By becoming soft and flexible, you are better able to handle stress, sustaining less damage. Also, your intuition will work better, flowing more freely. You will have the tools you need to transform unpleasant situations.

Further exercises could involve the observation of the chest, the breath, the jaw, and the shoulders, deciding consciously how you want to counteract the negative in life, instead of resorting to old patterns of reacting automatically to it. In stillness lies the power.

*Stage 2:* This will only work after you have experimented with stage one for a few days. You start out nearly the same way, but with two small differences:

1. You focus on your entire body.
2. You don't think of anything negative.

Concentrate on the biggest miracle that you can recall from your life. Breathe this feeling into each cell and store it there. Now, whenever you think of it, you can reactivate this feeling in your everyday life. For example, you can think of it while standing under trees, in the rain. This positive feeling will grow in your body, altering your perceptions, turning the mundane into the miraculous.

You have observed your body in a miraculous situation. With a little practice, those wonderful sensations will become ever stronger, available when you need them.

Now, you are again open to miracles.

A final thought on this topic: remember that miracles, like beauty, are in the eye of the beholder and have as much to do with novelty as with providence. Think about how a native of equatorial Africa might view snow for the first time, or how a brilliant young architect from the eighteenth century would react to the 3-D computer graphics of today.

Do not waste your energy begrudging the inexperienced their beginner's luck. Instead, focus on rediscovering the simple miracle of life. This will turn each day into a new beginning, and you can enjoy "beginner's luck" forevermore.

(Now, look at how irreverent this Barbel is! She doesn't even have respect for the unique character of beginner's luck. She actually wants to experience it forever! Doesn't this woman know any bounds? The answer is: No, why should I?)

# The Cosmic Ordering Service and Karma

Do cosmic orders disagree with the karmic laws of the universe? Well, I am actually not the best person to ask, for such worries go against my concept of the cosmic energy. Nonetheless, several folks have asked me this very question after attending my lectures, so I will do my best to dispel their concern.

To begin, let's make sure we are all on the same page: karma, as a concept, comes from the Indian renaissance teachings and stands for the sum of all good and bad actions from former lives. This final tally is carried into the present life, determining a person's fate. A track record of noble deeds produces good fortune, while an unsavory past generates an abject existence.

Suppose yours is a quite harrowing karma with much sorrow, mourning, and so on. And then, to add insult to injury, every time you have a day off, it rains. Naturally, you might say: "Poor, wretched human being that I am: I have only one day off every two weeks, and it just *has* to rain! How dreadful!" You sit in a corner and sulk.

Now, you could logically react this way, of course. However, despite all your unfavorable karma, you still have a choice. You could say to yourself: "Okay, fine; my one day off, and it rains! But if you think this is going to get the better of me, Universe, think again!" You then call your best friend, and the two of you hike across a beautiful landscape, whose attributes are not marred by the rain. Afterwards, you come home, turn on your favorite music, and take a relaxing hot bath with salts and lavender oil.

After your bath, you could make yourself a cup of hot chocolate or your favorite tea, open a box of cookies, and put your nose into the pages of a good book, listening to your favorite music with all your senses. Or you could pop in a DVD and watch a tearjerker.

Tearjerkers are always a good bet because the soul loves intense feelings, and if you block such feelings in the positive sense, the soul will create a few negative ones for you.

And so . . . hiking, bathing, drinking hot tea, eating cookies, reading or watching a movie . . . is that a bad day?

Admittedly, your bad karma ensures that it will rain on your only free day, but does that automatically make the day bad? Can you not choose to have just as good a day as someone with good karma?

Furthermore, can you not order from the universe what you believe to be your fate? Very probably.

The better the karma, the better the orders. The more good karma you have, the more comfortable you will be with ordering wealth. You already know the angle: everything that you don't need, you immediately receive because you are able to formulate the order with childlike innocence. You are not attached to it; therefore, you send it forth and forget about it. The more you become addicted to the illusion that you "need" this or that, the less likely you are to receive it.

The true power of your karma, therefore, lies in the way you allow it to shape both your expectations of your own life and your perceptions of what you need (e.g., beautiful weather on your day off).

Let's presume that, despite bad karma, you succeed in ordering one million dollars. This order, in light of your karma, is so absurd that you do everything right more by accident than by plan. Namely, you clearly formulate the order—almost as a joke—and merrily send it forth without giving it another thought. The universe obliges, delivering the million dollars to you. Now, here is where karma (i.e., your perceptions of your destiny) could come into play. Someone with positive karma would probably just accept the money, leaving it in his/her account for one year in order to become accustomed to it, to get used to the idea of being a millionaire. He/she would calmly evaluate all possibilities during that time, so as to make the best possible decisions. On the other hand, you—with your negative karma—feel so desperate for the money, so needy, you probably make a series of impulsive purchases, going through the money in a relatively short time with little left to show for it. Your opinion of who you are in the universal plan determines your behavior.

You can order that million dollars; you only need to do it with the same nonchalance as you would order a parking space in the center of town. However, whether it actually ends up being a good thing for you depends on your personality, your karma, and your thought life. The Cosmic Ordering Service delivers, but where you go from there determines your happiness. In the final analysis, it is your responsibility and yours alone.

Now, in such a case, here is the perfect order: "Dear Universe: I know that my karma is a catastrophe. I nevertheless order the necessary insight and self-knowledge to lead a happy life, despite my bad karma. Please deliver immediately and please, as well, schedule many repeat deliveries until I understand it. Thank you."

According to Varda Hasselmann and Frank Schmolke, co-authors of *Worlds of the Soul,* the soul has different ages, just like the physical body. There is a baby soul, a child soul, a pubescent soul, a mature soul, and an old soul. They believe that the soul matures to the next level simply through the passage of time, no matter what one does or does not do—just as a child automatically becomes an adolescent whether or not he is a "good child." In addition, each stage is equally interesting to the soul, affording the same potential for happiness, even though the actual experiences of each stage are quite different. For example, the pubescent souls are the ones who find it necessary to fight and wage war. Nevertheless, one can be content as a pubescent soul.

Pain and sorrow (again, according to Hasselmann and Schmolke) have nothing to do with bad karma or soul age, nor does their presence brand an entire lifetime as "wretched." Subconsciously, the human being has agreed that his/her development would benefit far more from sorrow than from happiness at this particular moment in time. That is possible in every soul age and with every karma.

Pain can bring more sensitivity, more love, and more understanding to a human being. One can realize these benefits regardless of his karma.

Also, it is important not to be too proud if one is very virtuous in this life, for this kind of extreme indicates a series of lives in glaring opposites. In other words, an intensely devout life this time around could make the soul feel that it fully understands this variation, and so, for the sake of experimentation, it could, in the next life, choose the exact opposite. By that same logic, an evil person in the current life could have been virtuous in his previous life, choosing evil this time, to come to a better understanding of it. Perhaps he will choose virtue in the next life.

And so, if it is all about choice, why can you not simply choose to order up a sunny day?

If your karma is really so bad that a simple, direct order like "Please allow my next day off to fall on a sunny day" can't work because you cannot believe in it, there are alternatives. For example: "Okay, Universe, I know that it always rains on my days off. However, I would like very much to enjoy the sun. Please show me an alternative way to enjoy the sun!"

Then, the universe could send you a colleague, who tells you that there is a wonderful park near your office. You negotiate with your boss to allow you to start work a half hour earlier and to stay a half hour later. You add this extra hour to your lunch break, which you can now spend in the park with your favorite colleagues, whom you inspired to make the same arrangements. In this way, your order for more sunshine is fulfilled!

Now, if you are more dogged, you might say to the universe: "Hey, Universe, my bad weather karma no longer interests me. Please send me an idea, immediately, how I can guarantee that my next day off will be filled with sunshine. I always catch the rain with my energy, but I want sun! Understood? I insist upon sun for the entire day!"

Perhaps nothing happens for several days, and you are about to resign yourself, but are nonetheless relaxed, as you walk to the bus stop in the rain. While you are waiting, your luckiest colleague drives by in his sports car. "Oh, there goes, Mr. Lucky," you mumble. Then, you recall: "On *his* days off, the sun always shines!" This person doesn't know anything else, for his inner attitude ensures that the sun will always shine for him.

All at once, the scales fall from your eyes. You simply need to go to your boss and apply for the same days off as Mr. Lucky! Time will tell whose karma is stronger: either Mr. Lucky will be reduced to rainy days, or you will be able to share in his sunshine.

"My goodness," you wonder, "why did I not get this idea before?"

The answer is simple: you never asked for it until now.

There is a story about a man who died and went to Heaven. Saint Peter showed him around, finally taking him to a wonderful villa where he would live now that he was in Heaven. The villa had everything: beautiful furniture, a splendid balcony with a magnificent view, a swimming pool, a sauna, a garden—simply everything a human could desire. There was only one strange detail:

"What are so many cartons doing in my living room?" the newcomer asked.

"Well," said Peter, "these are all the things that we had reserved for your earthly existence. However, you never asked for them, so we could not deliver them to you!"

There it is. You could inquire, at least once, what they are still holding for you.

You could even interpret the fact that you came across a book like this as good karma, or that I had the proper karma to order the writing of this book because your karma has arrived at exactly the right place to enable asking for the cartons that await you.

And whether you would like to be happy or unhappy when it rains is a matter of your mental attitude. You must also remember that opportunities are only given when the time is right.

In conclusion, it makes no more sense to try and force your spiritual development than it would to say to a five-year-old child: "Just grow up, already!"

Rather, you should recognize what makes you truly happy. Why devote every waking moment to work or to cerebral discussions about metaphysics if your soul would much rather play with other children in the sandbox? Give yourself, for at least one hour a day, something that really pleases you!

In so doing, you will find out more and more about who you really are and about what brings you true joy. You will discover that you discard more and more of the things that you only thought you wanted.

Begin, if you dare, with small orders and observe yourself: how do you handle the deliveries? Learn to be watchful and conscious in the present, learn to know yourself. Learn to alter the small things! Small and large are connected; therefore, the consistent altering of small things will have large consequences and will possibly dissolve all your karma in the end.

That is my opinion about it at least. You may have another. After all, a black and white printed opinion is worth no more than the ink and the paper.

# Is Ordering with the Universe Blasphemy?

I am frequently asked this question, along with others in a similar vein, such as: Who is the universe? Who runs the Cosmic Ordering Service? Is it God or some new idol? If the Cosmic Ordering Service is really God, is it not then irreverent to command God, to "order" him to carry out our wishes, as opposed to humbly asking? If it is not God, who or what is this omnipotent force? Is it one's "higher self," the "oversoul" of all people, an angel, or, perhaps, the subconscious?

To be completely honest: I don't know. I have a problem with the term "God," for it evokes a punitive, vengeful, masculine picture for me. The religious instruction I received as a child was largely responsible for this image. In fact, until rather recently, I was a strictly incredulous atheist. My philosophy was a materialistic and mechanistic one. I considered reports of miracles to be sheer nonsense—until I actually saw repeated examples of them. Then, I began to have experiences myself, that proved unequivocally that I had been mistaken. I was confronted with events that could not be explained mechanistically and that defied all natural laws.

This confused me; however, it also motivated me to begin exploring this alternate reality (if one could call it that).

Through this exploration, I have determined that I can talk to invisible forces and receive answers. Even more amazing, I can give up "orders" to these invisible forces and enjoy the manifestation of these wishes in my life.

"Ah, so, it does exist!" I said to myself, continuing my search for further evidence of this mysterious, invisible power. The Bible did not resonate with me, but many other books of a spiritual bent opened my eyes.

From divergent opinions, I only became more inspired, yet I could never look upon someone else's viewpoint as dogma. Even if a thousand other people accepted a teaching as truth merely because a guru pronounced it so, I needed to filter it through my own experience. Belief is a force that inspires further questing after belief.

The result of my personal quest—that you can freely discard or put on the shelf to explore at a later time—is as follows: there seems to be a force that creates everything, including humans. (Possibly, however, everyone creates themselves and manages to forget.) In any event, this force seems to have equipped each human being with creative power and a free will—as well as gigantic memory lapses, evidenced by the fact that almost no one recalls his/her origins as a soul.

I name this invisible authority the Cosmic Ordering Service because it is obviously a force that lies outside our physical reality, and it appears to be at least as large as the entire universe to me. I have discovered a kind of spiritual telephone, through which I can communicate my wishes to this force in the same way that one would order a pair of jeans from a mail-order company. My orders are then "delivered" promptly.

And so, this is the model that has been created for me. If one sticks to the "business conditions" in childlike innocence, immediately forgetting the order after placing it, yet remaining prepared to answer an "unknown phone," then, this service works extremely well. I invite you to call the Cosmic Ordering Service for yourself and formulate your own opinion.

If you don't have any problems with the word "God," good for you. What particularly bothers me about the whole concept is that many people who belong to a church, temple, or mosque have a fundamental view of themselves as "small and sinful." They may look upon any attempt to find something good about oneself as prideful or even blasphemous. They go through life with a humble reverence before God, content with life on the sidelines. None of this corresponds in any way with my view of creation.

The human being should be considered a sinner, while Almighty God is magnificence personified? I can't help wondering if the true blasphemy is in making myself so small and unworthy that I disparage God's own creation? It's like saying that the best he could manage is a group of poor, little sinners!

As I understand it, God is supposed to have created human beings after his own image. Therefore, it stands to reason that if he created poor little sinners after his own image, he must be a poor little sinner himself!

The longer I think about this theory, the more absurd it seems to me. God is supposed to have created the human being with definite abilities and the free will to make decisions about how best to use those abilities, but as soon as one exercises that free will, he is sent to Hell or otherwise punished.

In other words: the human being is created with enormous abilities, but the purpose of life is not to use them—or one will be punished. This sounds virtually sadistic to me! God would have needed to create only people who have no desire to break his laws. Why would he create the exact opposite and then punish them when they use the free will that he gave them in the first place?

This is not at all compatible with how I envision the omnipotent, universal consciousness.

On the other side of the coin, there are those that, in view of the condition of our world (hate, wars, and other horrific incidents), cannot believe in God or some other form of a higher power. How can such catastrophes happen on Earth, while this supposedly omnipotent force sits by and does nothing?

Do you know how? The higher consciousness gave us the power to solve all of our problems! However, by virtue of free will, we can decide whether or not to use our creative power.

As a former hardcore atheist, I consider it a fundamental error to pray in this manner: "Dear God, something must be done immediately about the poverty in this world. I cannot look upon it any longer. Please do something, God."

He (or the universe) already has: he gave you everything you need, namely creative power, after his own image. You can use your creativity to manifest—or even alter—anything you choose.

I find it much more fruitful to place a small order, such as: "Hello God or Universe, please send me the necessary intuition to recognize how I can eliminate poverty in the world. I would like to use my creativity in good will, initially, to improve my own life and, secondly, to improve the collective life on planet Earth. Thank you in advance. I know this is possible!"

If somebody views this "prayer" as presumptuous, then he has made himself small by questioning his creative power. What this really means is that he has a built-in excuse to do nothing: what can one poor, little sinner do about anything?

However, such excuses have no basis in fact. Anyone that recognizes his/her creative power can effect gigantic change!

Precisely on topic, one man has made so many efforts to eliminate poverty that, presently, he has already saved more than 10 percent of the entire population of his homeland, Bangladesh, from poverty. He is a shining example of what one human being can do on a world-wide scale if he believes in his creative power.

In 1976, Muhammad Yunus discovered that forty-two completely impoverished people in his neighboring village needed a collective total of only twenty-seven dollars to escape total poverty and become independent.

A woman, for example, manufactured bamboo chairs. Since she did not have twenty-two cents to purchase the bamboo, she had to borrow it from a money lender, who kept most of the profit. As a result, she only earned two cents per chair. Essentially, then, all she needed to become independent was twenty-two cents. The situation was similar for the other forty-one people in the village.

In fact, millions of people in Bangladesh worked for a pittance. And, of course, the poorest of these couldn't get credit from any bank. Not one dollar. Not twenty-two cents.

Muhammad Yunus gave this village twenty-seven dollars of credit, founding a bank for the poor. As of May 2006, his Grameen Bank has given more than four billion dollars of credit to millions of impoverished families. Always without collateral, he grants tiny loans of literally a few dollars. The bank now employs approximately eleven thousand people in more than forty thousand villages.

Interestingly, Yunus allocates approximately 95 percent of his loans to women because he has determined that the men of Bangladesh waste the money purchasing status symbols, while the families remain poor. The women, on the other hand, build meaningful businesses, and the repayment rate of the many female customers of the Grameen Bank is about 98 percent. No other bank in the world can compete with that.

Yunus's extraordinary efforts have inspired thousands in the Third World to follow his example, launching an entire system, known as micro-lending.

Whoever would like to learn more about how a single human being can accomplish so much should read Muhammad Yunus's memoir. (See recommended resources.)

Yunus was awarded the Nobel Peace Prize for 2006.

This inspiring story is only one example of the power an individual has to effect change. If you help yourself, then God helps you.

It does not seem to be particularly effective for one to portray himself as the poor, powerless sinner, who is dependent upon the grace of God to alter the world. "God helps those who help themselves" has been a popular saying for many years. This is an old wisdom, which I certainly did not invent.

Let's presume that there is a God in whom you believe. Which would please him more? Someone who did not ask for much, afraid of making himself too large, who piously praised the majesty of his creator every Sunday in church; or someone who would stand up and say: "What I see here, I don't like. I would like to improve the conditions in our world. I know that I can do it, and you, invisible power or God, can help me. I demand support to change both myself and the world at large!"

Clearly, the second "someone" could formulate his demand in a more reserved fashion. For example, the word "demand" could be followed by "in a way that is in unison with the divine will." This works well for those who are afraid of demanding something that is against the divine will.

Of course, if one believes that everything is God, this fear is not logical. However, logic is secondary. What is of primary importance is that one has a sense of well-being surrounding the order. In the end, everyone must decide for himself how best to communicate.

Personally, I need this nonchalant—and to many ears, irreverent—tone because I perceive these forces as having no higher universal rank than my next-door neighbor. It is easier for me to communicate my true desires when I "let myself go," not taking myself too seriously.

Now, I could speak with the universe in this manner: "Dear Universe, if it is convenient for you, would it be possible for you and I to be interconnected at this opportunity, so that the situation could change for the better. Please be so kind as to make this possible."

However, that would not be the right tack for me. It sounds too careful and too obsequious for me. This formula does not help me believe in my own creative power, and I must believe in this in order to succeed.

If one of my orders then arrives as a result of this belief, I usually dance through my entire apartment in mad glee, grateful for the miracles of this life. Clearly, it is more important for me to demand, to receive what I desire, and to feel grateful than to "pray" with formulaic politeness.

Too much politeness in dealings with the universe is suspect for me because one can easily cross the line into impotence or servility.

A human being that feels powerless and obsequious cannot create anything like the Grameen Bank. In order to achieve at this level, one needs to have the belief: "I can; I have the strength and the power to change whatever I choose."

Certainly, if you can feel the full extent of your creative power while speaking reverentially to the universe, you will also succeed. The key, here, is not to compromise your sense of well-being.

Perhaps a good suggestion is to talk to God or the universe as you would a close friend—someone whom you trust and who knows you completely. Such a person always understands what you mean, regardless of your tone of voice. Or even better: speak to the universe as you would talk to yourself. Think about how you talk to yourself while looking in the mirror. On some days, you feel the need to be especially kind to yourself. When you feel this way, address the universe in this manner.

However, on other days—and for me, these are more frequent!—you look into your face and reprimand: "Ah, we are sleeping through life, utilizing only 5 percent of our abilities! We deserve a kick in the pants to get us back on track."

On such days, I have the feeling that my universal—or internal—helpers are also sleeping, and so, I speak with them in the same tone I use on myself.

You should view God or the universe as your very best, most familiar friend or, perhaps, as your better half.

Many people also have the fear that it is not right if they order too much for themselves. After all, we must mostly think of the needs of others. Well, wonderful! If you think of others, your creative dialogue with your higher self will reveal the perfect order to benefit both you and the world at large.

In principle, your welfare is of great importance to the entire world. Why? Well, what did you think when I wrote above, that you should order intuition to show you how to eliminate poverty from our world? Perhaps you thought that I live in a fantasy world.

Or perhaps, you thought: "What can little old me do to make a dent in poverty? It is nonsense to think that I could have such creative power."

And then, what did you think as you read the example of Mr. Yunus, who created four billion dollars of credit from a mere twenty-seven dollars, freeing over 10 percent of the population of his homeland from total poverty?

If you are frustrated with your own life, when you hear of global problems, it is quite normal to think: "What can I do there? I can't even solve my own problems!"

However, after you have solved your own problems and simplified your life, you will experience many successes as your creative power becomes free to connect with the incomprehensible and invisible higher strengths. Then, someone will come to you with a wide-ranging problem. At this point, you will presumably think: "Ah, this is merely a problem, and experience teaches us that to every problem, there is a solution. Universe, what can I do to hear this solution? It would be my great joy to share this with everyone!"

To be sure, the universe could not imagine anything better than for YOU to become so happy that no problem of the world could intimidate you. Admittedly, you cannot solve all problems alone, all at once. After all, that would be unfair: other people need to have some fun solving a few problems!

Nonetheless, the happier you are, the more you appreciate your life, and the more eager you are to solve those problems that await you—and only you—to be solved.

Muhammad Yunus, for example, certainly has a capacity for fun, and he received great joy from reducing worldwide poverty. This is obvious from his memoir.

In addition, I had the opportunity to interview him after one of his lectures. He was such a jovial man, spreading so much humor and cheer that I simply had to laugh. He clearly demonstrated how much pleasure he derived from proving to the world that what seemed impossible was, in fact, quite possible.

At the same time, Yunus dreams in complete seriousness of being able to banish life-threatening poverty completely from the planet. Admittedly, this is still a giant step but again, not impossible.

To demand so much is not irreverent—quite the opposite. It actually shows respect for the abilities and opportunities that were given to you. By taking aggressive action to utilize these offerings instead of just allowing them to lie fallow, you are showing your true esteem for these gifts.

Now, here is a summary of the most important tips:

View the universal force in whatever way you like best: Cosmic Ordering Service, universe, God, inner voice, or intuition—it makes no difference.

Talk to the universe as you would to a completely familiar friend, or as you would talk to yourself.

Speak with the universe in such a way that makes you feel powerful. It is also important to use humor and to have fun.

If you believe in a deity, then operate under the presumption that he/she didn't botch the job but rather, equipped you with everything that you need in order to lead a happy and successful life. A nice bonus of your creative power is free will, which enables you to embark upon a new course at any moment.

Consider that it is perfectly logical for creation's purpose to be your happiness and your ability to manifest miracles, for if you create a paradise from your own life, you will be motivated to do the same for the rest of the world. Also, when life becomes joyful for you, you believe it is possible to contribute something meaningful to it.

If you cannot even clean up your own life, it is no surprise that you feel too powerless to help the world.

Consequently, it is not disrespectful to make great demands. On the contrary, it is the best thing you can do to help the world. If you demand much and have much, you can also give much. How can you give to others when you don't even have sufficient luck, joy, and sustenance for yourself?

How can you make the world a happier place when you project only misery? Radiate bliss and demand a lot of it— enough for the entire world! Then, you can devise a new plan to compete with that of Muhammad Yunus, which will even surpass his. I will assure you, he will be delighted to see it.

Take pleasure in everything that you have and receive. Acknowledge the smallest miracle, for gratitude attracts even more reasons to be grateful.

There is a beautiful wisdom that states: "Only the blind ask for miracles. The sighted recognize the wonderful everywhere they look."

And here's another: "The power of love is ubiquitous. However, what is not recognized, doesn't seem to exist."

Not to be grateful means not to see the miracles, and if they are not recognized, they do not exist. Gratitude is expressed by joy (as in wildly dancing around your apartment upon receipt of an order). This inspires the universe to sense something like this: "Ah, she truly liked this; therefore, we will immediately create more of the same."

As soon as you begin to notice miracles, the pervasiveness of them becomes clearer and clearer, until they turn up at every corner.

Hooray! One miracle a day, then two miracles a day, then . . .

The universe is also happy about this because if you experience multiple daily miracles, you will inevitably build up an excess that you will want to share. In this way, the universe has won one more voluntary helper!

The faster and the more you demand, the faster you generate excess and can turn into a helper. I speak not only of the quite mundane excess of money but of the excess of real inner fullness. Simply from the joy in being alive—and not from a need to be morally "good"—you desire to share your wealth and good fortune.

It is no fun to receive help from someone that has no real desire to give it. However, it feels wonderful when someone is happy to do whatever he can. *That* is a super feeling!

Spare your fellow men the ministrations that you do not enjoy bestowing. The energy that he/she receives on such an occasion feels more like punishment than a blessing.

Remember situations from your own life: how did you feel when someone helped you begrudgingly or simply out of obligation? Compare that to the feelings you experienced when someone was delighted—even considered it a privilege—to help you. Give others only the best of what you have experienced! To be able to do this, you must first give yourself only the best!

Therefore, if you want to be truly devout, you could consider, as true worship, the application of your immense powers to produce so much excess of luck and joy that you have an ample supply to share.

# Am I Even Worthy
## of So Much Joy?

That is the next typical question and one that is quite widespread. Almost everyone expresses feelings of unworthiness. Those who do not are usually suffering from megalomania. Even they, however, have noticed that something is not quite right and are just trying to hush up their internal cries of worthlessness. Someone once said: "Life does not need to earn the right to live. Life is a gift."

If you belong to one of the primary religions that teach the virtue of "making oneself small in the world," you probably see yourself as unworthy to live a beautiful life filled with ease. Through such perceptions, you are actually telling your God, indirectly, that his gift of life is not useful to you. How happy do you think that makes him?

The way I imagine it, you will come to God at the end of your life and say: "Hello, God, here I am again." God will then ask: "How did you like my gift of life? What did you build from it?" You will then reply: "Oh, you know, I didn't make much out of it. I always had the feeling that I was not worthy to do something truly great with my life."

Let's presume that your God is the Greek God, Zeus. At such a response, Zeus would no doubt erupt in fury, as expressed with thunder, lightning, and cloudbursts. He would yell: "What! You dare doubt one of my brilliant creations—namely, you? You have the audacity to openly say that I created something of no value!"

Zeus would perceive such self-deprecation as the utmost blasphemy: such insolence for a worm of a human being to criticize *his* infallible creations, even smoothly telling him that "Your creation, my life, was not particularly useful."

Now, luckily for you, the real God probably sees the matter differently, since he does not judge you and allows you to be as you are. But the Zeus of historic legend would have been mortally offended.

It often works this way in everyday dealings with other people. For example, go back in time to when you were a teenager . . .

Perhaps you are quite hot about a certain dress or suit; however, the garment is terribly expensive and is already sold out in your size. Now, maybe you have a headstrong aunt who is determined to move heaven and hell to give you this garment for your birthday. After an intensive search, she finds just the right garment in just the right size in another city, and there it is at your birthday table.

However, you—because you feel unworthy of such wonderful clothing—cannot bring yourself to wear the gift. And so, dusted with moth powder, protected in a plastic sack, it hangs in your closet, unused.

Sure, you thank your aunt many times for her thoughtfulness, but you also must admit to her that the dress or suit is much too beautiful for someone like you to wear. So, you hold the garment in a kind of place of honor, reserving a special place in your closet just for it.

How do you think your aunt would feel about that? Don't you think she would be hugely disappointed? She would not believe any of your noble-sounding words and would simply feel hurt because she would presume that you did not like her gift.

What would truly please your aunt would be for you to decorate yourself repeatedly with her gift, wearing it so often that it would completely wear out and disintegrate into dust.

I think, if there is a God, he would react similarly to your aunt. He is certainly much happier when you feel worthy to don the dress you truly want to wear, making your life extraordinary.

Essentially, it boils down to the same principle that I expressed in the previous chapter: if you do not feel worthy to give to yourself, you will have nothing of value to pass on to others. Whatever you do for others will be seeped in the negative energy of your unworthiness! You will have the aura of a human being that "does his duty," instead of living to spread true joy.

The old Zeus would, again, rebuke you immediately: "Not only do you downgrade my infallible creation—you—with your so-called 'humility,' but you also have the audacity to shortchange my other brilliant creations—namely your fellow man—with your inferior gifts."

Perhaps, in your determination to be miserable, you would attempt to point out that your "inferior gifts" are evidence of your unworthiness. Zeus wouldn't like that, either.

In fact, the only way that you should worship him is by praising his creation, visibly celebrating it daily, and acknowledging its value.

If you acknowledge *your* value and the wonderful and special in *you,* you are acknowledging the wonderful in the creation. That makes God, Zeus, and your aunt much happier.

I encourage you to prove this theory for yourself, using the following experiment. When you first wake up, look in the mirror and announce to yourself: "For one week, I am not worthy to accept answers from God, the universe, or the mental helpers." During that week, keep a record of how you feel. What kind of people do you meet? In what situations do you find yourself?

At the beginning of week two, stand before the mirror again. This time, however, announce: "I am worthy to lead the most beautiful, fullest life that I can imagine!" You can recite this before the mirror three times a day if it calms you, with the added bonus that this is a test to see what will make the divine happy and receptive to you. At the end of week two, compare the two weeks.

If God or the universe regards something as right for you, he/she informs you of this through a feeling of well-being. In which week did you feel better? In which week did you have nicer meetings and more beautiful experiences? In short, in which week did the Universe & Co. support you more by sending more beauty into your life?

Did they reward you for the "I-am-unworthy-week," or did they respond more favorably to you in the "I-am-the-crème-de-la-crème-week?"

Give my little experiment a try, and you will personally receive the answer from the Universe & Company!

## *Feel How You Really Feel!*

This is very important to me: I hope that, from reading one of my books, you do not get the stupid idea that you must be all smiles at every waking moment.

I was recently struck by this alarming concern while observing the participants of two different big-name seminars on positive thinking. They were completely independent events (one was German and one was American), each with several hundred participants. The strange thing that I noticed about both seminars was that a kind of mass phenomenon occurred. Apparently, many thought that in order to proclaim their enthusiasm for the contents of the seminar, they must constantly grin.

Even if they were not in the mood or just plain weary of it, they nevertheless grinned. Perhaps they were afraid that somebody would interpret their absence of a grin as being too stupid to comprehend the lecture. Or perhaps they were afraid of being labeled by the other grinners as not being a team player. Maybe they feared that the seminar leader could misinterpret the straight face as a criticism of his/her statements.

And so, in both seminars, the entire room grinned, no matter what. However, the group dynamic influenced a smile that was not too convincing. I did not have to look very hard to see how much energy this artificial joy cost its partakers: it only increased their fatigue, since it did not originate from the inside.

Neither of the two seminars actually stated that in order to practice positive thinking, one must assume a façade of eternal happiness. So, the need to do this must be an interpersonal phenomenon.

As I observed this phenomenon, I wondered what motivated these people to persist in it. They all appeared frantic to conform to any expectation in order to be accepted.

Once, I was with one of the organizers on the opening night of a three-day seminar, taking place in a luxurious hotel. All of the people there (or shall we say, *almost* all— after all, I was there . . .) were so self-important that it would have been completely pointless to smile at anyone. The collective aura was so cool and snooty that I began to wonder if I should do myself a favor and just leave. However, since I was already there, I decided to at least stay for the lecture.

The event began, and contrary to expectation, many high spiritual opinions and insights came from the podium. The speaker addressed both the false and the genuine aspects of life and how to distinguish one from the other by communicating with the true self. A change came over the room as folks began to realize that they really can decide for themselves what they truly want out of life, regardless of the opinions of others. The speaker radiated so much love and belief that I could sense a wave of relaxation moving through the rows. It was a feeling which seemed to say: "Ah, we are among friends."

During the break, it was apparent that the crowd dynamic had already changed. People tentatively smiled to themselves, then to one another, discovering that other people actually smiled back!

No doubt, they had carried their noses so highly in the air as a defense against rejection.

Now, they could talk to each other—and not only about the weather. Suddenly, extremely personal conversations transpired between people who had previously been strangers.

As a sense of trust develops, topics of conversation often become increasingly personal without effort—even when the participants scarcely know themselves, let alone each other. And it is usually safe to presume that anyone who sits through a soul-searching lecture without fleeing at the break is trustworthy.

It became even more obvious that their previously anti-social behavior had been motivated by insecurity and fear. Out of fear of being rejected, they had preemptively rejected others.

A popular theory that most of us took from our childhood is the idea that we could only be loved if we behaved a certain way. "If you are not good, I will no longer love you," may not have been verbally stated, but many of us came to believe that all the same. Since it is impossible to be "good" all the time, such a belief keeps us in a perpetual state of insecurity, treating love as a goal that needs to be continually met. (If I do this, my mother will love me; if I do that, my father will love me.) But what do we do if we simply want to be loved as we are? Then, it gets complicated. Due to the completely different conditions that the different people in our lives place upon us so we may remain "worthy" of love, we can barely assess our own needs. Of course, our logic tells us that to always be loved by everyone is impossible. Yet, love doesn't have anything to do with logic. It doesn't need any reason to exist; it simply is. Since however, almost no one knows this, most of us feel worthless from time to time, believing that it is vital to "earn" acknowledgment, admiration, and love from others. We are all too willing to hide our true selves in exchange for these attentions.

It all boils down to this: one often feels a little inferior, unable to fully accept what one is, namely "only" a human being that can be loved unconditionally. Then, one attends an event, such as the one described above, dealing with the liberation of the soul.

All at once, one learns that the only requirement is to go inward, looking to the self, to determine what is right, and that it is completely insignificant what Aunt Erma or anyone else thinks about how one should behave.

One looks around and sees others becoming more energized and open—no doubt enjoying the same enlightenment, the same awakening to self-awareness. As they become more self-aware, they become more confident, more amenable to intimacy. This group dynamic, in turn, energizes the individual, motivating one to do more with one's life. One recalls his dreams of youth, assessing which have been realized and which have not.

Small wonder then, if one desires to reach out to these new, vibrant people who obviously possess great promise. One becomes anxiously solicitous, hoping to make a good impression on them, since they seem so valuable. Quite logical and certainly understandable.

Then, some spiritual greenhorn need only come along and say offhandedly: "Why are you not in a mega-super good mood today?" And already, one hides behind the façade of a smile, afraid of not belonging. Thus, one achieves the exact opposite of one's goal and becomes stuck in an old behavior pattern: living as a stranger to oneself.

That is a normal emotional reflex. You need not terribly concern yourself should this happen to you. You are quite normal. You can, however, do yourself—and those around you who are also trying to return to their natural happiness—a favor by responding thusly to the misguided novice: "Well, my friend, you are probably afraid of not being accepted here if you don't smile all the time. I choose to treat myself better than that: I give myself permission to be honest to myself. True, I have bad days, but my constantly growing inner joy is so stable that it cannot be compared with your importunate, carnival mood. I trust that happiness will increase in my life at a rate that is right for me. I love myself unconditionally, exactly as I am right now. Relax, my friend, and feel how you really feel! The sky behind the clouds is always blue. As long as you remember this, there is no reason to deny that the clouds exist." (Of course, you could also express these sentiments somewhat more diplomatically, if you wish.)

Either way, after this philosophical gush, you can smile—genuinely—at your challenger, with the knowledge that you probably helped many an eavesdropper cast off the artificial self. Now, you can relax and feel relieved. Whenever you are truly yourself, you help not only yourself but others as well.

# The Sky behind the Clouds Is Always Blue

That is not only true of the heavens but also of our insides. Yet, humans differ greatly in the techniques used to reach—via the clouds—blue sky. Some attempt to work their way through the clouds (analyze, analyze, analyze); however, since they are directing their energy toward problems, they only reinforce them. Occasionally, such an approach can be fun or even meaningful for a short time. One must, as always, decide for oneself.

There is a more intelligent—or perhaps, just lazier!—approach: insolation, the deliberate, direct exposure to the sun's rays. In this way, the clouds simply dissolve, sparing one the entire "working through" process. However, this method also causes thunder and lightning. This does not seem very functional to me, unless one enjoys such adventure.

The attentive reader has no doubt discerned that I prefer to illuminate my sky with many, many suns, in the form of pleasant people, work that brings me joy, festivities, interactions with nature, and many other beautiful things that gladden my soul. With so much sun, the rain clouds cannot last long. Each year, they become sparser without my having to occupy myself with them. I find this method superior—solar dissolution of clouds as opposed to solar explosion: a slow, drying-out process as opposed to pushing out the front with stormy conditions.

I can still offer a small anecdote about my own cloudy sky for the sake of discussion: I had made a decision some time ago—which I admittedly do not regret—to face my own sorrow.

Someone once told me that trying to avoid sorrow only results in prolonging it. Nonetheless, this—like everything else—does depend on the personality. The melancholy type could obsess so much about trying to avoid sorrow that he thinks of little else, thereby protracting his misery. On the other hand, the more levelheaded type could shorten the duration of his suffering through tenacious efforts to expel it.

The melancholy type could certainly learn a thing or two from the second type about using distractions and undertakings to stay sane, instead of draping his windows in mourning.

I have always seen myself as a member of the levelheaded, second group, avoiding mourning my losses at all costs. So, it had been years since I had let myself feel as unhappy as I did at the time in question. Consequently, I was downright curious how deeply into the pit of despair I could fall if I allowed myself.

I had already come to the realization that "the sky behind the clouds is always blue," but exactly how dense were these clouds? In other words, what unresolved sorrows had I repressed that still had the power to hurt me? I decided to pursue the matter.

I draped my windows, turned off the phone ringer, and prepared for the worst. Fifteen minutes later, I was profoundly sorrowful. I recalled former situations in my life—from my school days and puberty—that had kept me depressed for days at a time. Nothing but pictures and feelings from these times—and from other equally depressing times—rose from within me.

Simultaneously however, I noticed, I no longer identified with these feeling and thought structures. Back then—prior to discovering the blue sky behind the clouds— I had believed in never-ending defeat. Back then, I had looked for escape, often feeling hopeless. Back then, I did not yet have any idea that I, without the approval of others, could install my own private sun by doing whatever stimulated my enthusiasm.

As I reviewed my moping memories, I suddenly realized how much better my life had become. The autonomy and self-knowledge that I had gained, along with the suns and the blue heaven, had led me to much more clarity and zest for life. Serious depression could no longer rise from within me. The clouds had become too thin. Fifteen minutes of mourning, and I was done with it—satisfied within my deepest self. I had been prepared to explore every psychic surprise, every regression, spending perhaps three days to determine whether the sun in me was real and not put-on or if I had just fallen prey to my own propaganda.

And what had happened? For a quarter of an hour, I had drawn comparisons between the past and the present, and all at once I felt removed from that woman who had covered her windows in solemn seriousness, in order to get involved in the bigger drama of herself. So, there I was, with an entire weekend stretched before me and all my dates canceled. I therefore decided to give this whole, deep, dark, probing thing another try. I prepared in total seriousness to look at my feelings honestly.

Approximately five minutes later, I was doubled over in a fit of laughter. The more I thought about myself, lying there with the windows covered in tragic seriousness, the harder I laughed.

After another fifteen minutes or so, I had laughed myself out. I pulled open the curtains, a friend called, and she and I went to dinner, spending an amusing evening together. I was completely finished with the mourning. It did not return.

Had I been afraid to face my own depths and the resultant emotional pain, this fear would have prolonged my mourning process considerably. These feelings surely would have been archived. Thus, by facing my self directly, I deleted those painful feelings from my hard drive and archives in fifteen minutes.

I hope this small sharing of my experience has helped you perceive how much a positive attitude can do if it is applied correctly. By steadily projecting positive beliefs, you thin out the cloud layer, until it becomes too feeble to "rain on your parade." Even when those clouds cast a shadow, they are so thin that you can easily poke your head right through them to view the blue heaven on the other side.

As in the inscription on the oracle of Delphi, the most important component is: know yourself. If your cloud layer is sixty kilometers thick (real clouds in the sky can allegedly pile up this high), then it is in your best interest to rush head-first into the darkest feelings that you can uncover.

The key to everything: know yourself. Nothing else really counts. No matter what tools I share with you, no matter what has helped me. If you are hyperactive, more silence is the next important step for you. If you sulk motionlessly in a corner of the room, the next important step for you would be more movement—dancing, running, playing ball, whatever. What harms one person heals another. Who can ever truly know exactly what you need besides you?

To know yourself is the most important step. Be more honest with yourself each and every day!

Also, it is impossible to be too strict with yourself. Once, I was so brutally honest to myself that I felt terrible afterwards. I had admitted all my worst characteristics to myself. It was an honest moment of self-assessment, but I felt dreadful about it.

I immediately placed an order with the universe: "Universe, please do something to cheer me up!" A book from my shelf suddenly called out to me. I walked over to the bookcase, pulled the book from the shelf, and allowed the pages to fall open to the phrase: "You have not discovered real truth if love does not grow from it!" (Hans Kruppa's *Book of Spells*).

Ah, self-love had by no means increased through my honest recognition. Therefore, upon further reflection, I discovered a higher truth, which likewise stimulated my love for myself to grow.

# *Final Thoughts*

You can simplify your life with one, all-encompassing order: order a personal paradise on Earth! Stand before a mirror, look into your eyes, and converse with yourself until you are convinced that you deserve it and that the best path is the one upon which you can most effectively influence the entire world with your joy.

You cannot give what you do not have. Therefore, you must have luck and joy in order to give it to others.

Moreover, all that you require is a little self-awareness, so that you know what makes you truly happy. Then you will not pursue the wrong goals.

If, on the first try, your orders with the universe do not work out, then all you should conclude is that you need more practice to make it work. And in the meantime, illuminate your sky with as many suns as you can find. Thin the clouds that weigh upon your soul until they are nothing but pretty, little, white flakes. Then, your all-encompassing order for a personal paradise on Earth can manifest, and you can spread the joy—the creative joy—from which one finds a solution to every problem. After all, problems do not exist to be dismissed but to be solved.

The better you do in life, the better you become at solving problems. Therefore, you are justified in ordering a heavenly life from the universe!

Know yourself! Play around with this until it works out! Order that your entire life transforms more and more into a paradise on Earth. Consider that if thousands of people ordered this, the planet would have little choice but to become a complete paradise!

*Everyone Is a Luck-Smith*
*He knocks at the door, and I ask: who is there?*
*I am luck, he softly replies.*
*Luck—I think, I spin—*
*will you let me in?*


*I am sorry, but*
*I do not have the time for luck.*
*I have so many things to do*
*that I cannot postpone.*
*Thus no luck here can I allow.*
*One cannot be lucky always, anyhow!*
*Luck often comes unexpectedly,*
*but if it cannot come when I am free,*
*it had better stop misfortune!*

—Helmut Gebhard, singer-songwriter from Tenerife
(his lyrics mostly pertain to his own life and his own beliefs)


P.S. Now and then, readers that seem to believe write and ask if I am somehow singularly clever or enlightened. I then wonder if they have really read *The Cosmic Ordering Service*. Otherwise, how could they mistake me for someone who is singularly clever—with everything that I get myself into? Do me a favor and forget this nonsense! It does not gratify me, for my message is completely the opposite: If I, a completely average lunatic, can give orders to the universe without end and thereby receive so many improbable things, then YOU can, too! This is what you should take away from my successes.

# Recommended Resources

Gebhard, Helmut (singer-songwriter from Tenerife). His CD and/or lyric sheets are available from: Isabella Sunday, Seestr. 54, D-86938. Fax: 08192-934257 or from Helmut's daughter via telephone: 06324-980777. Helmut goes on tour for several weeks at a time and is always pleased when someone can arrange further opportunities. He loves performing in nursing homes and hospitals. He has a completed musical, for which he needs a good manager.

Jasmuheen. *Living on Light* (KOHA Publishing. ISBN 3-929512-35-1). This book details the twenty-one-day process that anyone can use to free the body from dependence on food. It contains statistics and scientific results.

Kaiser, Karina. Reverse Speech practitioner and trainer. Website: www.reversespeechinternational.com; email: karina@reversespeechinternational.com.

Kensington, Ella. *Mary* (available only in German; can be ordered from Günther Vaas, Munich, Tel. 08091-563871, fax 563872).

McMoneagle, Joseph. *Mind Trek: Exploring Consciousness, Time, and Space through Remote Viewing* (Hampton Roads Publishing. ISBN 1-878901-72-9). This is the definitive book on remote viewing, written by a participant in the United States government's remote viewing program.

Oates, David, founder of Reverse Speech. Website: www.reversespeech.com.

Yunus, Muhammad. *Banker to the Poor, Micro-Lending and the Battle against World Poverty* (Public Affairs, 2003. ISBN 978-1586481988).

# About the Author
## and Translator

*Barbel Mohr* has published twelve self-help and children's books in German, including the best-selling *The Cosmic Ordering Service,* which has sold more than one million copies in Germany alone and has been translated into fifteen other languages. The book recently exploded across England after Noel Edmonds, popular host of *Deal or No Deal,* revealed how following the principles in *The Cosmic Ordering Service* changed his life. Mohr originally wrote the book for a small group of friends, distributing it as photocopies, before Omega-Verlag agreed to publish the version that became a best-seller.

Born in Bonn, Germany in 1964, Mohr has worked as a self-employed photographer, editor, graphic artist, and video producer. From 1995 to 2001, she traveled widely in Germany to promote better living through her seminars and lectures, including a workshop, "How to Have More Fun in Your Daily Life." The birth of her twins in 2001 has curtailed her public appearances.

Anything else worth knowing about the author and *Cosmic Ordering* can be found at her website: http://www.baerbelmohr.de/english/index

*Dawn Bailiff* received graduate degrees from the University of Vienna, Austria in technical translation and philosophy, where she specialized in the writings of Rudolph Steiner. While there, she wrote *Using Music to Teach Math, Foreign Language, and Technical Skills: Incorporating the Anthroposophic Principles of Rudolph Steiner* (published in German). Her translations of Rudolph Steiner, G. W. F. Hegel, and Martin Heidegger have appeared in numerous journals including: *New View, The German Quarterly,* and *Paideia.* She also does technical translations for major corporations.

Formerly a world-class concert pianist, Bailiff performed with such major symphonies as Berlin, Vienna, London, Seattle, and Los Angeles. Also a composer, her opera, *Anblicke des Himmels und der Hölle* (for which she wrote the libretto in German) was performed in Berlin, Dresden, and Stuttgart.

Bailiff's poetry and fiction have received national and international acclaim. Her metaphysical memoir, *Notes from a Minor Key,* is scheduled for release in Fall 2007 by Hampton Roads Publishing Company.